OFFER IT!

This book is written for all women who may be size-challenged (fat), chronologically-challenged (old), or gender challenged (female). We may be those things (as irrelevant as they are), but we also have resources, education, connections, time, maturity, and experience. We have something to offer. (Girl, do we ever!) The world is in darkness and despair and there is need everywhere we look. Let me be clear: **We have something to offer**. And we need to offer it. If we do, we can make a huge difference.

Fat Old White Ladies* are being called forth. We are a sleeping giant and God is awakening us for such a time as this.

*(& Fat Old Asian Ladies, & Thin Old White Ladies, & Fat Old Black Ladies, &...)

So I'm a
Fat Old White Lady
I can still make a difference

Fat Old White Lady. Copyright 2015 by Frances E. French-Marcott. All rights reserved. Printed in the United States of America. This book or any portion thereof may not be reproduced or used in any manner whatsoever without the express written permission of the publisher, except for the use of brief quotations in a book review.
Published in Central New York, USA
First printing 2015
Art of Thriving Publishing
ArtofThriving.net

Cover design by FEF Marcott

ISBN-13:
978-0692517475 (Art of Thriving Publishing)

ISBN-10:
0692517472

Except when noted, all Scriptures are taken from the Holy Bible, New International Version®, NIV®. Copyright © 1973, 1978, 1984, 2011 by Biblica, Inc.™ Used by permission of Zondervan. All rights reserved worldwide. www.zondervan.com The "NIV" and "New International Version" are trademarks registered in the United States Patent and Trademark Office by Biblica, Inc.™

When noted, Scripture quotations from THE MESSAGE. Copyright © by Eugene H. Peterson 1993, 1994, 1995, 1996, 2000, 2001, 2002. Used by permission of Tyndale House Publishers, Inc.

So I'm a
FAT OLD WHITE LADY
I can still make a difference

by
FEF Marcott

Art of Thriving Publishing
Central New York

TABLE OF CONTENTS

Section One: Getting Started 1
    1: Introduction: What's In A Book? 3
    Core Principle: God Sets All Things Right 7
    2: Barnyard FOWL 11
    3: Murder Most FOWL 19
    Core Principle: God's Big Dream 25
        Section One Workbook 29
Section Two: Repair 33
    Core Principle: Healing the Wounded Heart 35
    4: FOWL Smell 41
    5: FOWL Yourself 45
    6: FOWL Language 49
    7: FOWL Deeds 57
    8: FOWL Weather 61
    9: Cute Chick 65
    10: FOWL Things Up 69
        Section Two Workbook 77
Section Three: Growth 83
    Core Principle: Treasures of Darkness 85
    11: FOWL Fritters 93
    12: FOWL Air 97
    13: Birds of a Feather 101
    14: Perfect FOWL 107
    15: Under the Shelter of His Wing 111
        Section Three Workbook 117
Section Four: Service 123
    Core Principle: On God's team 125

16: Well-Fed FOWL 129
17: Feathering Your Nest 131
18: The Roost 133
19: Water FOWL 137
20: Laying the Golden Egg 141
    Section Four Workbook 153
    What's Next 157
    Appendix: About God 158
    Appendix: About Us 159
    Ordering 160
    The FOWL Forum 161

SECTION ONE: GETTING STARTED

I am excited that you have picked up this book. I have prayed for you that, as you read it, you will capture a vision of what God is doing—and could be doing through you and other women like you. I have such hopes that something deep in your heart will begin to stir, resonating with the moving of the Holy Spirit as He works in us all to accomplish His purposes in this day and at this time.

Fat Old White Lady

1: INTRODUCTION: WHAT'S IN A BOOK?

Is there ever a time when we are of no more use, when have "spoiled," gone beyond our "expiration date," and can only be thrown out with the trash?

Are we done yet?

For those of us in middle age or older, there are many signs telling us that we've entered a new season of life. We've raised our kids, had our career for (how???) many years. Young adults start looking younger and younger. Our bodies are in the middle of or have finished their menopause thing, with all the many joys of those changes. (Yeah, I'm kidding.) And so we start to wonder if we are done. If maybe we should start to think about wrapping it up.

And those of us who are long past that phase of life, who are now—no getting around it—*old*, have maybe even quit wondering and just decided that, yes, we *are* done; we have nothing left to give.

This book is an emphatic NO! to that notion! The idea that we older women are done is certainly the message we've received for years. But it is a false message and we need to see it as the blatant lie it is! We're not finished until we're finished. We don't need to be done until God says we're done. And God doesn't let age, grown kids, life stages, or physical bodily changes dictate His love for us, the strength of our faith—*or* our suitability for His service.

This book is for at least five kinds of women:

- One woman has been so damaged, so hurt by the circumstances, people, or events of her life that she doesn't believe she has any worth. She has done very little self-development and practices very little self-nourishing. She lives with severe self-loathing and depths of emotional pain. She couldn't imagine that she has anything to contribute.
- The second woman is the one who has decided that she is done. She has raised her kids, she has worked hard and is now retired, and she can do whatever she wants because life is all about her now. She is going to have *fun*. She doesn't care to contribute.
- The third woman has a busy life, is active in her church, is competent, and reasonably healthy as a person. But it has never occurred to her that God might have a specific purpose for her to fulfill. She never considered that God might have called her, uniquely and personally, to contribute.
- The fourth woman lives aimlessly, purposelessly; pretty much just waiting to die. Life is about medical issues, limited finances, irritating neighbors, and a good gossip session with the girls each week over cards. The idea of having a purpose has never been a part of her thinking. In fact, God doesn't factor much into her thinking, even if she goes to church fairly regularly. The idea that she—even at this later time in her life—could make a contribution is as foreign as speaking an alien language.
- The fifth woman has been dismissed and ignored. Although she has experience, training, competence, and gifts that she is willing and able to offer, she has still not been seen for who she truly is, how valuable she is. She has been sidelined because of how others see (or don't see) her—fat and old and female. She isn't given the opportunity to contribute.

What's in a name?

This book is for women of a "certain" age. Most definitely, this book isn't just for *white* women. I'm hoping a variety of women will find that this book speaks to them—especially middle-aged and older women. I myself am a FOWL (Fat Old White Lady) so that is where I started.

What's here?

This isn't a long book. It is meant to be an overview, not going into great depth on any one topic. I have written or can recommend other books, as well as my blog and video courses, that offer more detailed information on some of these topics.[1] This book is meant to get you thinking in a different direction. To be a call that says, "Wake up! Get going! You're not done yet." If you finish this book excited that you *aren't* finished yet, with a vision for what might be possible, then I've accomplished what I hoped for.

Most chapter titles are meant to engage the title of the book. Fat Old White Lady abbreviates to FOWL. So many chapter titles are puns and word plays on *foul* or *fowl* or are related to birds somehow. I apologize to all older women who are not fat or white, but the play on words doesn't work with any other combination. Bear with me!

This book has 20 very short chapters. Each one covers a different aspect of how to prevent the fact that you are a FOWL (or FOAL, or TOWL, or FOBL)[2] from stopping you from being everything that you can be. You might have been guilty of murder most FOWL. You may be exuding a FOWL smell. We've all smelled it and sometimes it starts with us. You might spend too much time watching for FOWL weather. I've done that, and you probably have, too. You'll learn what benefits could be found in flocking together with birds of a feather.

---

[1] See last pages at the back of the book for a description of these resources
[2] Fat Old Asian Lady, Thin Old White Lady, Fat Old Black Lady

You'll learn to identify the symptoms of the Good Girl Syndrome and what an alternative lifestyle might look like. And you'll be reminded to rest in the Roost.

At the beginning of each of four main sections, there is a Core Principle. These Principles are the foundation behind everything I have written here; the reason why I write this book. If you can grasp these truths about who God is and His ways, they will revolutionize your life like they did mine.

At the end of each section is a workbook with exercises that I hope will be useful for your own personal growth. Some of the questions might also be helpful for discussion in a small group setting. (Those are highlighted in grey.) In addition, you can download some "road maps" (step-by-step guidelines), worksheets, and other helpful resources from the artofthriving.net website. If you are not online, you can receive these by mail. There are directions for doing this in the final pages of this book.

I offer a number of Scripture references throughout the book. Like most Christians, I consider the Bible my authority on matters of God, Christ, the Holy Spirit, the Church, life, and faith. So I share the Scriptural support for the points I make whenever I can. You can find those in the footnotes. These are worth studying.

How to read this book

I hope that you will listen with your heart; hear the truth, feel the way it speaks to something deep inside of you.

I also hope that you will listen with an open mind. Let go of your preconceived notions about who you are and what you are capable of. Be open to God speaking something new to you.

In the chapter following the first Core Principle, I will tell you why I wrote the book and how the idea of "fat old white lady" got started.

CORE PRINCIPLE: GOD SETS ALL THINGS RIGHT

God has always had a plan to set things right. He didn't leave us floundering in this mess.

The original Creation which God made was perfect and whole, gorgeous and complete. Once sin entered the world through the actions of Adam and Eve,[3] He could have turned His back, washed His hands of us in disgust. But, instead, He has been working ever since to make it right.

He is no APITS

I was attending a class when I heard the term the *Missio Dei* for the first time. Even though it sounds like an ancient Latin term, it was coined only recently.[4] It means "the Mission of God." Hearing about it changed my life. Up until then, without really examining it, I saw God as the Angry Parent in the Sky (APITS) waiting to punish me if I got it wrong. I believed He was always unhappy with me, and that He expected me to obey Him perfectly, but offered no help to do so. I was on my own to both figure out what He wanted and then make that happen — without screwing up. (Because if I screwed up, He was

---
[3] Genesis 3
[4] 1934 by Karl Hartenstein and revived again in 1991 by David Bosch.

just waiting to punish me, but good!)

But then I heard about the *Missio Dei* — God's plan to set everything right. To fix what is broken, heal what is sick, find what is lost, lift up what has been beaten down, free what is in bondage.[5] Basically, the *Missio Dei* is God's work to bring about shalom. (More on that in the next Core Principle.) He has a Plan and has been working that Plan. That's the kind of God He is. God is the Lord of the *Missio Dei*.

It blew me away. That didn't sound like the Angry Parent in the Sky! That changed everything for me. This is the kind of God I could fall in love with. This God I could serve with my whole heart. He is a Good God.

It matters how we see and understand God; what we think of His character and nature. In the parable of the talents[6], the three servants had very different understandings of the master. The first two went eagerly to work. Their positive attitude toward the master was justified by his reaction to their work. He was not only pleased. He actually promoted servants one and two to partners! The third servant used his negative impression of the master to justify his own inactivity. The lazy, wicked servant did what he did (or didn't do), in part, because he didn't know the true nature of the master. The other two did, however, and their bold steps of faith and their efforts were well rewarded. Many of our choices come about because of our understanding of and relationship to God.

The Center, the Axis, the Main Thing

Scriptures tells us that there will come a time when God judges the whole world, and everything that isn't approved by Him will be punished, and even burned up with fire.[7] But Scriptures are also clear

---

[5] Isaiah 61:1-4
[6] Matthew 25:14-30
[7] Matthew 25:31-46; Revelations 20:12-13

that God redeems, restores, and transforms; He doesn't throw away.[8] Because I saw God as the APITS, it was easy to focus on judgment, whereas now that I know and love the Lord of the *Missio Dei*, I can see God's work of healing and restoring all around me. This is the season of redemption and restoration, rescue and renewal. The whole world is invited to get in on it.

God is the center of all things, the axis around which everything else revolves. The *Missio Dei* is the main work going on. You've heard the adage: *The main thing is to keep the Main Thing the main thing*. Well, the *Missio Dei* is most definitely the most Main Thing there is or ever was or will be!

---

[8] Psalm 103:1-5; Isaiah 53:5; Luke 4:18-21; John 3:16

Fat Old White Lady

2: BARNYARD FOWL

The world does not take middle aged and older women seriously. All too often, we don't even take ourselves seriously! We come to accept the belief that there are certain things we are good for—and not much else. Farmers grow chickens for their eggs and also as meat. Those chickens might not be worth more than that, but this book is here to say that *we* are worth far more than doing the housework and cooking the meals. It is time we stood up and were counted as an essential part of God's plan.

Woman One

I mentioned in the first chapter that I am writing for at least five kinds of women. One is so beat up or has such low self-esteem that she feels that she has nothing to offer. I attended a women's retreat one winter. There was a woman there who hardly ever made eye contact with anyone. She was overweight and the way she dressed showed that she didn't think well of herself. She had done nothing that helped herself look or feel attractive.

From her demeanor and manner, I wondered if she had been abused as a girl and/or if her husband had not been kind to or supportive of her as an adult. This woman attended church services and most church events faithfully. She was the kind of woman who could always be counted on to help in the kitchen or set up the church rummage sale—to serve. But she never took on leadership because she had no self-confidence. She didn't think she had anything to offer. In fact, she was convinced that she was worthless.

Woman Two

I know of a woman who is bright and talented. She has had an interesting career in the corporate world. She and her husband were able, through good financial management, to retire in their fifties. They travel, do extensive work on their beautiful house and garden, take interesting self-fulfillment classes for adults, and go to and host parties. I am thrilled for her that she has such a wonderful life.

But I also always grieve that she has so much to offer through her work experience and education (she has an MBA) but all that wealth and resources are having no impact on the world. There are places that need the kind of help she could bring, but which could never afford her experience and skills. She doesn't need to be paid because she has a sufficient retirement income. And she is such a cool person. It breaks my heart that all that she is and all that she can give isn't being offered somewhere. She has decided not to bother.

Woman Three

She was in a weekly prayer group. She had been faithfully attending, and she clearly had a heart for God and His Kingdom. She had served in more than one way at her church over the years, and had even, upon occasion, been in church leadership. Yet, when the leader of the prayer group asked the group if they knew what their purpose in life was, what God had called them to do—she had no idea. In fact, she had never considered the idea that God might have called her to something specific.

Because she never asked the question, she never listened for the answer.

2: Barnyard FOWL

Woman Four

She doesn't work anymore. (In fact, she is of that generation where the woman quite often did not work outside the home.) Her husband has been dead for years. She has very little money and lives in low-income housing. She pays nosy attention to her neighbors. (Their lives are far more interesting than hers!) She endlessly watches TV: cooking shows, soap operas, reality shows. She saves up and occasionally joins a seniors' trip to the closest casino where she makes a cup of quarters last all day. She doesn't sleep much anymore, she lives far away from family, so she has lots of long, empty days. Yet it has never crossed her mind that God might have something else for her; that her small life was actually meant to be lived large and full of love.

Woman Five: My story (and why I wrote this book)

I will say up front that my work experiences are somewhat unique. You might not relate to what I have done as jobs, but I hope that you can still relate, nonetheless, to the *type* of experiences I've had *in* those jobs.

I am ordained and, at the time of this writing, have served as a pastor of five churches. I knew from the time I was in 4th grade, when I felt God speak to me, that I would be a leader in the Church. For a long time, the only notion I had of the shape that this call would take was the role of pastor. The modern North American Church doesn't acknowledge a breadth of church leadership roles. We primarily have the position of pastor or missionary, even though there are several other leadership roles mentioned in Scripture.[9] For years I told the leaders (all men) of the churches I attended that I felt called to church leadership. None of them encouraged me or told me what I needed to do to accomplish that goal. When I finally worked on staff for a female

---

[9] Ephesians 4:11-12—Apostle, Prophet, Evangelist, Pastor, and Teacher. Timothy 3:1-10 Overseer and deacon

pastor, she not only recognized my call, but laid out for me the steps to get there, and encouraged me to start the process. As a result, I went to seminary rather late in life.

There, I discovered a particular kind of church leadership called church planting—starting new churches from scratch. After having been in established, traditional (dare I declare them "stuck-in-the-mud"?) churches all my life, starting from scratch sounded wonderful. Maybe we could get it right from the very beginning. Be about the community around us, not about the building. About making a difference in the world, not about us and our comfort. Not spectators in an audience, but motivated and gifted servant-leaders effecting a difference in the world. Wow, that sounded great! I have gifts as an entrepreneur and project manager so the idea of starting a church felt perfect for my abilities and passions.

I made a number of attempts to be a new church planter with more than one denomination. However, I absolutely could not get any traction! One reason was that, in the denominational region I was in while in seminary and first working as a pastor, the regional leadership didn't believe women should even be in church leadership. They were not willing to work with me and they found excuses to write me off. This happened more than once.

Then, through a city pastors' group I attended, I came across a different denomination. The pastors from that group talked all the time about how dynamic it was, how they were planting churches all over the place and doing that really well. It sounded like it could be the right place for me. So I went through their church planter discernment process. It was pretty rigorous, with extensive interviews and assessments (personality inventories and questionnaires).

During the course of the application and vetting process, my husband and I were invited to the region's annual conference. Over the weekend, there were breakaway groups for special interest or training. One of the groups was for church planters, folks who were currently planting new churches in the region, or about to. The director with whom I had been working through the application process led the group and invited me to attend.

It was pretty funny. My husband and I were in our mid-50s — there with 33 young men in their thirties. There was a whole lot of piercings, tattoos, spiked hair, and retro-geek eyeglasses in that group! My husband and I stood out like sore thumbs. We were introduced to them as being in the discernment track for new church planting. None of them said anything but the look on their faces was stunned. Huh? What?

Eventually, my husband and I made it all the way through to the final stage of discernment. All the finalists came together for a weekend with a discernment team (leaders from the region) who conducted interviews with each of us. We did planning and communication exercises while the discernment team watched. They were trying to get a handle on whether they thought that each of us finalists were indeed called to new church planting.

At the end, the discernment team did not accept me as a church planter. I was shocked — and broken-hearted. I had been sure that I was called to church planting. So sure — that I was not at all prepared to be told no. It took me quite a while to get over the shock and the grief; to figure out where to go from there.

Months later, I was still trying to process the experience. So I called the director I had worked with and asked him to tell me again why I wasn't accepted. He said something about what the discernment team thought I could or couldn't do. I felt then (and still feel) that they were very wrong about me. I was capable of and qualified to do what it took. And, even if I *was* missing an essential skill, they could have trained me in what I was missing. Or they could have teamed me up with someone who had that skill and we could have done it together. My point is that there were options to pursue if they had actually desired to keep me.

I told him, "You primarily didn't accept me because I am a fat, old, white lady, right?" I give him credit—he about swallowed his tongue when I said that. He protested that of course that wasn't the reason.

But I remember sitting in that conference with all those young, male church planters. If they were the denomination's standard, I knew that they simply couldn't see *me* as a new church planter. It didn't matter how good I was at what I did, how experienced I was, how many gifts I had that made me suitable, or the brilliance of my ideas—I was a fat, old, white lady, and they could not see me belonging among their shiny young church planters.

This occasion was not the only time I was dismissed for being a FOWL. Even though most mainline denominations have theoretically been ordaining women as pastors for years, in very many instances, local churches don't seem to have gotten that memo. If they have *any* choice in the matter, they will choose a man as their pastor every time.

And in the churches where I did serve as pastor, the congregations had a hard time seeing me as a leader. I came into one church where the previous pastor had served for a long time with a very different leadership style than mine. He was much more autocratic and domineering, whereas I came in as a collaborator, doing a lot of research and listening before making any decision, involving others to work as a team, and working hard to make decisions everyone could support. Several people in the church saw this as weakness because it was so contrary to their previous experience.

I usually attended the weekly or monthly pastor gatherings in each place that I served. It was rare to have a male pastor treat me as an equal. In one location, while I was still new at pastoring, I tried to be active in and supportive of the local pastor group. It was always very clear that most of my fellow pastors considered me a "junior" member of the group.

I'm not really complaining. Yes, it hurt. Yes, it was annoying. But I am mostly just observing that people usually see the fat, old, white, and female part of me—all of which are descriptive words for superficial characteristics—and see nothing else. They act as if those characteristics completely and exhaustively define me!

If you see yourself in one of the five women described earlier in this chapter (or another that isn't here), maybe you would like to rewrite the ending to your story. Instead of being too wounded, too self-absorbed, to unsuspecting, too disconnected, or too misunderstood, maybe you would like to reframe yourself. This book would like to help you do that.

Dreaming is an essential skill for the process of reframing. If you have never dared to dream, or you dreamt a long time ago but not lately, the next chapter is for you.

Fat Old White Lady

3: MURDER MOST FOWL

You might be guilty of having killed your dreams. Of having died to your deep desires.

Dreams are hope

The truth is, when we have a dream in our heart and ignore, dismiss, or avoid it—we kill it. And when we kill it, we are actually dying to life itself. Because dreams are fuel, dreams are hope. Hope drives us onward and upward.

It is important to have goals. Goals give focus to our lives. They keep us moving in a positive direction. Dreams are the "deep why" behind the goals. Dreams are the fuel burning in the engine of forward progress.

We all miss out

Not only do each of us need the hope and fuel of dreams, but when we die to our dreams, to those deep heart desires, those dreams are never given to the world, and the world misses out.

I truly believe that the deepest dreams of our hearts find their source in God, that He is the One who has planted them there. And when we kill them or never give them birth at all, we keep them—not only from the good they could do in our own lives—but the good that they could do in and for the world. I believe that they come from God and He wants us to pursue them.

But He gives us a choice. We can choose not to pursue them—and He will let that happen.

I knew a woman who, in the course of her years teaching, had come up with a way to teach math to young children that was revolutionary. No one had ever seen it before. It would have been extraordinarily effective for the many children who struggle with learning math, getting them started off well. She has this dream, and she has even collected tools for years with which to teach it. But she has never done anything with it. Nothing at all! This remarkable teaching method that God gave her is not being shared with the world.

You may also have answers to some of our world's most vexing problems. An idea you have might be a solution that would change many people's lives for the better. What you know or can do could make a real difference—but only if you offer it.

Extraordinary

God not only gives dreams, He has also given gifts to help us accomplish these dreams. These would make everything in the world better. Because that is the kind of God He is. That is who He is. That's what He can do.

However, He bestows these gifts on people. He endows us, providing us with the opportunity to make a difference. When we don't, we miss out and the world misses out. When God entrusts us with these dreams, these deep passions in our hearts, they are meant to make us extraordinary, and to make an extraordinary contribution to the world.

I have a friend who is, by nature, an introvert. She likes routine, she keeps her head down, she is pretty mild-mannered. She has always had a heart for the child who needs a home, who needs a loving parent. In addition to raising nine terrific children of her own, over the years she has also fostered four other children at her own expense, including, for several years, a brother and sister. I think she has the spiritual gift of mothering. Now that her children are nearly all adults, more independent or out of the home, she has been exploring what comes next for herself. She has been learning more about the global orphan crisis. When she talks about what she is learning and how she might start to contribute to the solution, she gets downright fiery. Her passion is all over this. She has already begun working in this area by making a presentation at her church for Compassion International (and she *hates* public speaking!). She has already begun making an impact, and I am eager to see what will come in the future.

One of my favorite quotes ever is: *The place God calls you to is where your deep gladness and the world's deep need meet.*[10] Our dreams are our deep gladness and they have the potential to make a huge difference to the deep pain and need of the world.

Permission to come aboard

Permission granted, ma'am! You can't wait for someone else to ask you for your help, for your idea, for your participation. Unfortunately, that probably isn't ever going to happen. No one is going to beg you to contribute. If you are going to contribute, you are going to have to *offer* it, to step forward, even push yourself into the midst of things.

Our culture practices blatant ageism—the one prejudice that no one seems to protest much against. It often appears that the world around us automatically considers age or disability to equate to stupidity and ignorance! Is that true? No! Of course not.

---

[10] Buechner, Frederick. *Wishful Thinking: A Theological ABC.* New York: Harper Row, 1973.

I was doing an online search for books in the same genre as this book. I didn't find many. I was frankly appalled by what I *did* find. Most books were for caregivers of older folks and talked about getting them to exercise, dealing with dementia, socialization, and other "old age" problems. I found almost nothing urging seniors to continue to contribute.

Yes, as we age, some of us do face truly difficult (and sometime insurmountable) health challenges. Getting old is not for the faint of heart. The challenges can be daunting. But they don't have to define us!

I have had a chronic condition for many years. It started with one issue, which then developed into a "cascade" of other conditions over the years. It means I experience chronic pain, chronic fatigue, and other unpleasantness. If I stayed in bed every time I felt bad, I would be semi-invalid! I have chosen not to be defined by or dictated to by my health. It isn't easy, but I am not giving up on my life, on making a contribution before I am finished here! I think we all have to make that sort of choice. Like the lazy servant, in the parable, there is always something that could be a reason for not getting involved.

Why not?

The woman I mentioned above with the math idea was soul damaged. (There is more on this in the chapter *FOWL Smell*.) She was wounded as a child and as an adult. She has never been able to truly get past her past. That damage kept her from realizing her full potential and from birthing her dream.

If we have a dream that we have never pursued, we need to ask ourselves why. What is it that has kept us from moving forward?

There are a lot of reasons why we may not have gone after this dream:

- When we were a child, someone told us that we were stupid, or that we would never amount to anything—and we believed it.
- We told one of our dreams to someone, and that person (probably an authority figure) poo-pooed it; told us it was ridiculous, that we'd never do that. And we believed them.
- We did try once, but we didn't succeed, so we gave up.
- We told ourselves, "Someone like me could never achieve that."
- Maybe we didn't know how to go about pursuing it.
- The idea of actually accomplishing it felt terrifying.
- We've made everyone and everything else more important than us, so we never got around to it.
- Because it is something we wanted to do so badly, we automatically assumed that it must have been selfish (because of course we can't possibly get to do what we most want to do).

Low self-esteem. Hurtful experiences. Life circumstances. Rejection. It is important that we look at the reasons we didn't move forward. Bring them before the Lord and ask Him what He wants to do about them.

Whatever it might be, there *is* a reason that we have killed our dreams. Anything that stands in the way of us accomplishing God's will is *not* God's will! It is destruction. It is evil. It is sin. Anything that stands in the way of doing what God calls us to do needs to be addressed.

And we are not on our own. We get to partner with God. (More on this in *Core Principle: On God's Team*.) We get the opportunity to carry out this dream that we hold in our hearts—*with God!* Do you have a dream? You must pursue it!

Fat Old White Lady

CORE PRINCIPLE: GOD'S BIG DREAM

Did you know that God has a dream?

It's a good one!

It is *shalom* over all the earth. Shalom is a wonderful word in Hebrew that means **wholeness, prosperity, peace, health, safety, well-being, favor.** That is what God wants for His whole creation. His desire is that the whole world live in shalom. Jesus is the Prince of Peace.[11] Our English versions translate the word as peace, but it is shalom, which is peace—and so much more. This shalom is another way of describing the Kingdom of God. Everywhere the rule and reign of Christ is—there will be shalom.

God wants to set everything right. He wants to make all things well and whole. That was what Creation was like originally. This is because God is good. He wants the best for all of His Creation and He wants that for each of us.

Once I realized that this was God's Big Dream, it has become my own pursuit. I want to establish it in my own life and I want to work with God to establish it in the world.

---

[11] Isaiah 9:6

What shalom looks like in our lives

Jesus talked all the time about the Kingdom of God, mostly through parables and stories. Any time He began teaching with, "The Kingdom of God is like…"[12] He was giving an illustration that helped to explain a deep truth about the Kingdom, this realm where the shalom of God reigns.

Thriving is a quality of life

Shalom is given by God, but it must be desired, invited, and cultivated. It doesn't happen by accident. It is so different from the world around us that we have to be trained to live in it. When we live in shalom, we thrive. We experience:

- *Love.* We have relationships which are well-tended. We give and get forgiveness as often as is needed, and we spend the most time with those who matter the most. The relational debris between us and others has been addressed and dealt with. We have deep and abiding relationships with the people who are significant to us.
- *Liberality.* We understand the joy of "blessed to be a blessing."[13] We don't cling to possessions nor are we owned by them, but instead, we share freely and generously to meet the needs of others. Our attitude toward money isn't driven by fear or greed, but by gratitude.
- *Integrity.* We do quality work at our jobs and in our other responsibilities. We are honest and reliable in all our dealings, and we keep our word.
- *Equilibrium.* We withstand problems, trials, temptations, and difficulties with dignity and a positive attitude.
- *Hope.* We look forward to our future. We anticipate the improvement which growth will bring. We have seen what good has happened, so we know what good can come.

---

[12] Matthew 13:31, 33, 44, 47
[13] Genesis 22:17-18

- *Harmony*. Harmony is agreement, a pleasing arrangement of parts. When we attend to ourselves, our environment, and our relationships — in as much as it depends on us — bringing them into health and order, we create a harmony of the parts of our lives.
- *Fulfillment*. We are living up to our potential, we are expressing our passion in our work, we are exercising our talents, and we are able to focus the most time and energy on what we most love doing.
- *Gratitude*. We understand that every good thing is a gift, and we are thankful.
- *Joy*. Because of all of these qualities, we have joy — not always happiness, which is based on circumstances — but something much deeper and more permanent.[14]

Dare to believe

As you can see, shalom is wonderful. Who wouldn't want it shaping their lives; who wouldn't want to live in it? No matter how fabulous it sounds, shalom is not a pipe dream or a fantasy — because it is God's declared intention. God operates in truth, not fantasy.

There is no bigger goal than God's dream to establish shalom over all the earth! We are invited to participate in establishing God's shalom. That is a big dream we can sink our teeth into, something we can get excited about pursuing! We can dedicate our lives toward that goal. We can work with God to establish shalom in our own lives and then beyond us in the world.

---

[14] Marcott, FEF. *Art of Thriving: 12 Life Skills for Personal Transformation* (to be published soon). Used with permission.

Fat Old White Lady

A workbook for this first section follows (and after each of the remaining sections). There are questions that apply to each chapter of the section. The questions highlighted in grey might be particularly good for discussion in a small group.

SECTION ONE WORKBOOK

What's in a Book?

1. The chapter described five different women. Do you see yourself in one or more of the women described?

    ❑ She couldn't imagine that she has anything to contribute.

    ❑ She doesn't care to contribute.

    ❑ She never considered that God might call her personally and specifically to contribute.

    ❑ The idea of making a contribution is totally alien.

    ❑ She isn't given the opportunity to contribute.

    Why do you see yourself in that particular example? Are you willing to have that view challenged or changed?

2. Are there other types of women who fit into the FOWL list?

Core Principle: God Sets All Things Right

3. Had you ever heard of *The Missio Dei* before? How does it affect your faith to know that God has always had a Plan and been working that Plan? Can you list ways in which you have seen God's Plan, the *Missio Dei*, in action?

4. I mentioned that my broken, messed-up view of God was *The Angry Parent in the Sky*. Did you or do you have your own misunderstanding of God? Look at the Scriptures about God in the Appendix. Does your understanding of God jibe with those, or do you need to do some work on your understanding of who God is?

6. Is God the *Main Thing* in your life? What about His Kingdom? If not, why not? Do you need to make any changes?

Barnyard FOWL

7. Do you agree that our culture doesn't take FOWLs seriously? Have you experienced that? What happened? How did you respond?
8. Have you had an experience where being a FOWL (or related and similar acronyms) affected the way you were treated? What happened? How did it make you feel? Did it impact the way you moved forward? Is there something your response that you need to change now?
9. Do you believe that you have anything to offer? If not, why not? If yes, have you already offered it or not yet? What is preventing you from offering it now?

Murder Most FOWL

10. Have you had a dream that you never birthed? What was your reason(s) for not doing so? What do you think of the notion that killing your dream is a form of murder? How does it make you feel that your dream is dead? Could you resurrect and do it even now? If you think not, why not? What is stopping you? Is the thing that you think is an obstacle truly an obstacle—one that could withstand your determination and hope empowered by God?
11. I shared a quote from Frederick Buechner: *The place God calls you to is where your deep gladness and the world's deep need meet.* What do you think of this statement? Does it ring true to you? Have you ever worked in such a way? That is, where your deep gladness was meeting the world's deep need? Can you identify a place of need right now that your deep gladness would love to touch? Can you step forward to do that?

13. Did you find yourself in my list of reasons for why you never pursued your dream?
    - ❏ When you were a child, someone told you that you were stupid, or that you would never amount to anything.
    - ❏ You told one of your dreams to someone, and that person (probably an authority figure) poo-pooed it; told you it was ridiculous.
    - ❏ You did try, once, but it didn't succeed, so you gave up.
    - ❏ You told yourself, "Someone like me could never achieve that."
    - ❏ Maybe you didn't know how to go about pursuing it.
    - ❏ The idea of actually accomplishing it feels terrifying.
    - ❏ You've made everyone and everything else more important so you never got around to it.
    - ❏ Because it is something you want to do so badly you assume that it must be selfish (because you can't possibly get to do what you most want to do).

    If you checked any of the boxes, what are you going to do about it?

14. Do you have a Big Dream? What is it? Are you doing anything about it? If not, why not? What do you need to do to get started? Make a point to share your Big Dream with another person. Pray together about it. Ask God to give you insight as to how you might still do it.

Core Principle: God's Big Dream

15. What do you think of the description of God's Big Dream as being shalom? How does that idea make you feel?
16. Have you ever experienced shalom: **wholeness, prosperity, peace, health, safety, favor, wellbeing?** What was it like? Are you praying for God's shalom to cover the earth? What could you do to make God's Big Dream *your* Big Dream?

18. Evaluate your life from the perspective of the description of shalom. How does your life measure up? Where could you make changes to bring shalom into your life?
19. What could you do to spread shalom around in your own little corner of the world? Pick one element of the description and begin to work there. Make a plan. Take your first step.

SECTION TWO: REPAIR

If we are going to step up and begin to make a difference, contribute to something of eternal importance—there are some things that need to be addressed. We need to take a look at ourselves. Is there anything holding us back? Are there attitudes, issues, brokenness, or dysfunction that are keeping us from being everything and doing everything God created us to be and do? This next section takes a look at some of those issues. I hope the Core Principle will deeply encourage you as you examine the state of your heart and face what you need to work on.

Fat Old White Lady

CORE PRINCIPLE: HEALING THE WOUNDED HEART

Healing the wounds of our souls is necessary, is possible—and is available even now.

About damage

If we have been hurt by the behavior and choices of another person, if we have experienced a difficult or traumatic event, if we have made mistakes or choices that have not turned out well—we have sustained damage to our souls. It is the human condition; most of us have it or have had it. Damage in our hearts gets between us and God, us and others, us and our true selves, inhibiting our ability to function.

Soul pain results in turmoil, confusion, depression, and myriad other negative emotional states. Damage can result in acting out (as in anger), "acting in" (as in self-harm), and other dysfunctional behavior and choices that harm us or others.

Sozo

Sozo is a wonderful Greek word that is often translated in the

Bible as "saved." Its full meaning is **_healing, deliverance, and salvation._**[15] It is the word used to describe what we have, what God freely gives us in Christ Jesus.

Sozo is available to all of us. If you love the idea of shalom over all the earth, *sozo* in individual lives is what will make that possible.

Sozo of the heart

The wonderful news is that God heals the wounded heart. One of my very favorite verses is in Isaiah. *The Spirit of the Sovereign Lord is on me, because the Lord has anointed me to proclaim good news to the poor. He has sent me to **bind up the brokenhearted,** to proclaim freedom for the captives and release from darkness for the prisoners, to proclaim the year of the Lord's favor and the day of vengeance of our God, to comfort all who mourn, and provide for those who grieve in Zion – to bestow on them a crown of beauty instead of ashes, the oil of joy instead of mourning, and a garment of praise instead of a spirit of despair.*[16] (Emphasis mine) It is the Messiah's "mission statement." Jesus quotes from it at the beginning of His ministry.[17] In it, one of things we are told that He is going to do is "bind up the broken hearted."

Is that cool or what! One of the specific ministries of Christ is to heal the wounded heart!

U-turn

If we are going to receive this *sozo*, we will need to stop the destructive behaviors that are causing us harm. Both John the Baptist,[18] and then Jesus' disciples, when Jesus sent them out, preached the need for radical life change.[19] This is repentance, making a U-turn in the direction of our lives.

---

[15] Romans 10:13; Ephesians 2:8
[16] Isaiah 61:1-3
[17] Luke 4:18-19 (Read it also in The Message)
[18] Acts 19:4 (The Message)
[19] Mark 6:12-13 (The Message)

Repentance means we stop doing the bad stuff, the wrong stuff, the harmful stuff. It is something that God does in us and also something that we choose and do ourselves. The radical life-change will mean *sozo* will be possible in our lives. (Obviously, we can't be healed and made new if we keep operating in the exact same way we always have, continuing to do all the things that have brought us harm. Remember the definition of insanity: To keep doing the same thing in the same way—but expecting different results.)

Once we've repented, made that U-turn, then we can receive healing of our broken heart.

The pursuit of healing

If we have damage, we need to be healed. Healing doesn't happen by accident. We have to recognize the hurt for what it is. We have to intentionally pursue healing. We have to participate in our healing. It we don't, the pain won't get better! In fact, most of the time, pain will attract or cause even more pain.

But we don't have to live that way. We can be healed.

Healing is a process; it happens in stages, and likely will continue for our whole life. We need to make the effort to progress toward wholeness. (I've been actively pursuing it since I was 19 and am not done yet. But I am vastly more healed than I was back then!)

The cool thing about learning the skills of getting healed is that we can use those skills, not just for healing the hurts of the past, but healing from anything that life throws at us as we go (because life happens). It is an incredibly valuable life skill.

About healing

Healing begins with ***acknowledging the pain***. We need to recognize the damage in our hearts. The thing that is truly amazing to me is that so many people go through their lives in pain and dysfunction without ever recognizing it as brokenness. I see this as I walk through my grocery store. Person after person looks so beat up, so broken, so downtrodden! In our broken world, it might be normal to hurt, but it is not necessary. Not with God.

Next, we need to **decide that we want to be healed**. We can cling to our pain, but we can also choose to let it go. Healing doesn't happen by accident; it takes intention.

If we see our damage and want to be healed, we must take steps; we must **enter the process of healing**. Being healed of our damage doesn't happen instantly, it is not easy, and it is rarely a pain-free process. And it is a long-term commitment. It takes action, perseverance, and dedication. (A road map describing the healing process is available from Art of Thriving. See the final pages at the back of this book.)

But the good news is: when the broken parts are addressed, the pain decreases, the dysfunctional behavior clears up, and we have the ability to enter into and sustain healthy relationships, and function in life in a healthy way. This means improvement in every area of our lives. Going through the healing process is worth everything it takes!

How to be healed

Our participation. As mentioned above, healing demands our intention. If we are willing, over time, God will bring us everything we need for healing. But we have to pursue it. We have to work with the process.

Tools. We can't possibly get healed without outside input and help. There are some tools that help make healing possible. These tools include:

- *Resources.* Books and teaching by others with experience and healing of their own, professionals with well-researched insights, conferences and seminars, bible studies, sermons. There are lots of resources that offer help and insight for the issues we face. We need to avail ourselves of them.

- *Journaling*. Reflection is essential to healing. (Not to be confused with introspection or rumination.) We need to be self-aware and mindful. A journal helps us to understand ourselves better, see our issues more clearly, and to track our progress. There are specific journaling techniques that can actually help us to dig into our soul where the damage lies and excavate it.[20] Journaling can also be a way to pray that helps us stay focused. You can download my free journaling "road map" (steps to effective and healing journaling) on my website www.artofthriving.net.
- *Counseling*. This provides perspective from outside of ourselves, the benefits of the counselor's knowledge and experience, and the helpful resources to which they can direct us.
- *Support groups*. Meeting with people who are all dealing with the same issue, people who have suffered similarly to us and are in their own healing process, can be powerfully instructive, encouraging, and empowering.
- *Community*. We all need to be loved; we need to be in relationship, to know and be known. Being loved and accepted is incredibly healing. Being with people who love us for who we are (not what we can do for them) is essential to our healing. No woman is an island and no woman can heal in a vacuum.

The power of the Holy Spirit. Jesus told us that the Holy Spirit is given to God's people to comfort, teach, guide,[21] and empower.[22] The Holy Spirit is the power of God at work in our lives. He helps us see and understand, He does the healing work in our hearts. Yes, of course, anyone can find a degree of healing without God's involvement. But God created us and knows us intimately. He is also loving, perfect, all powerful, and good. He knows what we need in order to heal and grow. If we yield to His work in us, He can bring about

---

[20] Cameron, Julia. *The Artist's Way: A Spiritual Path to Higher Creativity*. NY, NY: Putnam, 1992. See her discussion of morning pages, pg. 9.
[21] John 14:16
[22] Acts 1:8

deeper and more thorough healing than we can even imagine.

Transforming Prayer. This is healing prayer ministered to us by the Body of Christ in His name, motivated and directed by the Holy Spirit. In transforming prayer, the supernatural gifts of the Holy Spirit are released through human prayer ministers: words of knowledge, encouragement, wisdom, healing, and more. God speaks and works through His yielded servants to minister healing. It is very powerful. Growth and healing increase exponentially when the Holy Spirit works through God's people.

I urge you to pursue *sozo* — salvation, healing, and deliverance — as hard as you can. It is totally worth having.

4: FOWL SMELL

I think you'd agree that most people like bananas. A delicious, beneficial fruit; harmless—until the banana peel sits too long in the garbage! Then it truly stinks! I'm terrible about letting science experiments grow in my fridge. I open the lid of a container and about pass out from the smell.

Did you know that the rotten garbage in the basement of your soul stinks, too? It needs to be dealt with.

Must and can

If our heart has been broken, if there is some pain or damage sitting in there rotting away, if there is a resentment that is constantly burning (and giving off a stench like a burning pile of old rubber car tires)—we will not be able to move forward. Our soul's damage, and the negative heart attitudes we have developed must be dealt with.

I had a job experience that ended really badly. I was fired for no apparent reason. The way they handled me was unfair, unjust, and unrighteous. (And they were allegedly a Christian organization.) For months I struggled with healing from the pain. I tried to move forward with my life, starting a new business, but I kept running up against internal resistance. One day it occurred to me that maybe I didn't have closure with that job, so therefore, I wasn't free to move forward.

As I began to explore that notion, one day in my quiet time, I came across a scripture in Luke. *To you who are ready for the truth, I say this: Love your enemies. Let them bring out the best in you, not the worst. When someone gives you a hard time, respond with the energies of prayer for that person. If someone slaps you in the face, stand there and take it. If someone grabs your shirt, giftwrap your best coat and make a present of it. If someone takes unfair advantage of you, use the occasion to practice the servant life. No more tit-for-tat stuff. Live generously.*[23] Reading that, I realized that I had not been responding to what had been done to me the way I should have been, in the way Jesus wanted me to. In fact, I was harboring some pretty nasty attitudes like unforgiveness, resentment, judgment, retribution, and even hatred.

The ridiculous part of this was that none of those attitudes were doing a *thing* to the people about whom I felt them! Have you heard this adage: *Unforgiveness is like drinking poison and expecting the other person to die.* The unforgiveness and other bad attitudes weren't hurting them; they were only sitting there in *my* heart, smelling and feeling gross. They were sin — *my* sin.

God wants to heal our hearts. We can't function at optimum capacity if our heart still hurts or if we are entertaining destructive emotions and attitudes. That rotten garbage in our soul will prevent us from being fully who we were meant to be. It will affect everything we do, hindering our relationships, our forward progress, and our ministry.

Where damage comes from

The damage can come from an almost infinite variety of sources. We live in a broken world, we have an enemy of our souls, and we

---

[23] Luke 6:27-30 (The Message)

ourselves have a nature that is wayward and doesn't always make the best or right choices. The hurts can come through any and all of these. There are many different kinds of woundedness. Just a few examples:

- *Self-hate.* Feeling so badly about ourselves, having such low self-esteem, that we never take care of ourselves — not eat properly, nor clean our house, nor wear clean or nice clothes, nor go after good jobs — because we don't think we deserve it.
- *Projection.* Being so angry at the way our father treated us that we reject *every* man — boss, friend, or potential mate. I knew a guy who was angry at his mom, but he could never direct his anger to her. So, like stepping on a ketchup packet, he squirted sideways, and anyone around him could receive random blasts of his anger. If an authority figure said something to him, he would vomit anger all over them in reaction. He lost numerous jobs because of this. His current boss wasn't really the problem. It was anger against his mother projected onto any authority figure that came along. His anger poured out of his heart in all sorts of inappropriate ways.
- *Downward spiral.* We know this story. It is repeated over and over in our world. A woman is sexually molested as a child. She grows up to be promiscuous. Sleeps with too many inappropriate men and a lot of them hurt her. She begins to take drugs to self-medicate because it is all so painful. She feels stuck and doesn't know how to get out of it. More men hurt her. Eventually her drug use isn't self-medicating, it is a full-blown addiction. She starts to sell herself in prostitution to pay for the drugs she is using. Her entire life got utterly out of control and it all began with her wounded heart.

The thing about heart pain is that it usually brings about *more* damage and pain. An original hurt leads to one bad decision after another. You've seen how a pot hole in a street that isn't repaired gets bigger as car after car goes over it. Each car digs it deeper. In the same way, with behavior sourced in our damage, each bad decision is repeating and continuing and increasing the hurt. Acting out of the original pain, not thinking clearly or healthily, we can make bad choices. As with most bad choices, these cause *additional* hurt.

Not only that, but wherever we are hurt, we are more vulnerable to being hurt again. New damage in a place that was already injured will hurt even worse than it normally would have because it is already wounded. If you are already feeling stupid because your boyfriend derides you, if you made a significant mistake at work, you are going to take that more to heart because you already felt bad.

So you have another hurt to carry around. This downward progression can continue indefinitely.

Don't stay this way

We need to know that God wants to heal us. Healing the wounded heart is what God does. That means that walking around with a wounded heart is so unnecessary! This is one of my deepest passions, my heart cries: To tell people that if they would only deal with the pain in their hearts, they could move forward, live well, know God's love, and be effective and productive in their lives and ministry.

I urge you to be healed. Don't go another minute with pain you aren't facing and dealing with. Please don't go to your grave still wounded. That would be such an unnecessary waste. Deal with your broken heart.

5: FOWL YOURSELF

When we see ourselves as worthless, as rubbish, then typically we don't practice good self-care. Lack of good self-care is FOWLing ourselves. We know the Golden Rule: *Treat one another as we want to be treated.*[24] And Jesus' command: *Love one another as I have loved you.*[25] Love is to be the core of every relationship. That includes our relationships with ourselves.

Part of coming into maturity, part of being healthy and well-balanced, is the ability to take good care of ourselves. To practice appropriate self-nurture.

Care of all the parts

We are a triune being: we have a body, soul, and spirit.

- ***Body***: our physical substance. Our five senses, systems (circulatory, endocrine), structure (skins, skeleton), appearance, and strength.
- ***Soul***: the seat of our will, emotions, intellect, personality, and talents.
- ***Spirit***: our eternal being. It is the part of us in connection with the spiritual realm. When we are a believer, our spirit is alive

---
[24] Matthew 7:12
[25] John 13:34

to God. God is at work in us through our spirit. Our spirit hears from God, is nurtured by the presence of the Holy Spirit.

Good self-care is needed in all three areas of our life. If we do not love ourselves or take care of ourselves, we are actually in opposition to the will and ways of God!

- Self-care for our bodies. We already know the drill: eat a good diet, exercise, get enough sleep, reduce stress, go to the doctor as needed, take necessary meds, clean it, moisturize it, and brush its teeth every day.
- Self-care for our soul includes keeping our mind active and continuing to learn; striving for increased self-understanding; pursuing the gifts we have and developing them; developing our interests and passions; developing good character attributes.
- Self-care for our spirit: Develop our spiritual life. Be in communication with God, listening to and pouring out our hearts to Him in worship and prayer. Read and study Scripture. Practice spiritual disciplines. Pursue holiness and purity.

In proper order

We need to learn how to keep soul and body in alignment with and submitted to our spirit. We mustn't think our mind is the highest part of us. Human reason isn't the highest thing—God is. Besides that, we can't rely on our minds to do the right thing. They are as infected by sin as the rest of us. If God is Lord of our lives, He resides in our spirits. Our spirits need to lead our three-part nature.

Certainly our body should not dominate.[26] Yes, we need to practice good self-care, but we don't need to idolize our bodies. We don't need to spend a fortune and a lot of our time and effort on trying to maintain an illusion of youth and beauty. We need to put most of our time and energy into that which is immortal (our souls and spirits),

---

[26] 1 Corinthians 9:27

not into something that, no matter how hard we try, is still going to end up in the grave. (More on that in *Cute Chick*.)

Getting started

If you have neglected an area of your life, take small steps to begin setting it right.

A significant area of self-care has to do with our words. We cover that in the next chapter.

I invite you to read my other material. You'll find more information on how to have a quiet time with God, how to journal, and other tools and practices of self-care. See the artofthriving.net website or the final pages of this book for more information on these resources.

6: FOWL LANGUAGE

There are words that hurt, that destroy, that can change our life — and not for the better. These words can come from others and they can come from ourselves. They are FOWL language and they need to stop.

What's in a word?

Those terrible, negative things that people have said to us are not the truth. The way they have treated us isn't right. And yet, what they have said and done has shaped and constrained and oppressed us more than we can imagine.

I had a friend Jane who was raised in a very abusive, messed-up family. Her mom preferred her brother to her and told her so many times over the years. At one point, Jane's brother was dying of cancer. Her mom said to Jane, "I wish *you* were dying, not him." This awful, painful treatment had gone all her years growing up and continued into adulthood.

Jane always felt like she was "less than." She never got any sense of worth or value from either her mother or father. Jane's mother was a wounded mess. Out of her mess she hurt her daughter. It wasn't until Jane came into a relationship with Christ and started to understand that God loved her unconditionally—so much that He sent His own perfect Son to make it possible for her to be forgiven and reconciled to Him—that she began to appropriate the truth that God spoke to her. Jane began to heal. God's love and truth began to replace the lies, to turn around the devastation that had been caused by her family of origin and upbringing.

The problem with authority

Negative messages can also come from other people in our lives besides our parents, especially authority figures like teachers, coaches, pastors, or bosses. Authority figures in our lives have an incredible power to speak into us. They can alter the course of our life by the things they say to us—both for good or ill. If our dad was fond of saying, "You're an idiot, you'll never amount to much," as a girl, we internalized that and believed it about ourselves. If someone said, "You're ugly." Or, "I don't want you. No one loves you." that can stay with us. Little girls believe those words. It goes deep into our spirits and we can carry that pain into adulthood.

Other people may have originally said those terrible things to us, but the biggest problem is when we say them to ourselves. We receive it, believe it, and repeat it to ourselves. Then we act out the fruit of those words in our lives. These hateful things we say to ourselves keep us wounded and disabled. What we might have learned as a child, we continue to enact in adulthood, doing it over and over and over. This will characterize the rest of our lives—unless we do something about it.

I was broken and dysfunctional in a number of ways. I had an abusive authority figure in my life. I was sexually molested as a child by a family member. These and other things had caused damage in my heart. I had very low self-esteem and a lot of self-doubt. Even though I was smart and gifted, I didn't do much with those gifts. I didn't believe in myself or my abilities.

This point of view manifested in the way I spoke to myself; my inner voice. One day, when I was running on the jogging track, I was self-conscious because there was another young woman running who was far more fit—and beautiful—than me. I realized a little voice like an imp sitting on my shoulder was constantly spewing really awful things into my ear. "You look retarded." "Speed up, you loser." "They are going to think you are fat and lazy." How awful!

Once I saw it, I could start working to change it.

Sourcing the hurt

The negative messages can also come into our hearts and minds from the traumatic things we've been through. Any hard, painful experience (event or circumstance) can be a source of our hurt.

I had a friend who shared about a childhood experience that scarred him for much of his young adult life. He was born blind into a poor family. When he returned from the school for the blind to his family, there was no room in the small house. The house was already full with many children, plus some grandchildren. He had to sleep on the floor in a sleeping bag. There was no closet space so he had to keep his belongings in a garbage bag. His young soul interpreted this as meaning that he had no worth or value. He carried that sense of self-hatred and low self-esteem for many years.

It wasn't until he was able to understand the context that he was able to come to peace with that circumstance and release the hurt. (His single mother was poor and there were a lot of kids, but she did everything she could to hold the family together. It was only circumstances, never a statement of his worth.)

The APITS

It is also possible that we have made what people have said about and to us more important than what God has said. Who God says we are, how God feels about us, how delighted He is in us — *that is truth*. We need to know, repeat, and remember what God says about us. (In the Appendix, I have listed some of the scriptures that tells us what God thinks about us.)

As I mentioned in the *Core Principle: Healing the Wounded Heart*, for a long time, I thought that God was the Angry Parent in the Sky. He was just waiting for me to get it wrong so that He could knock my block off. I thought that a lot of the negative messages that my heart was hearing and believing came from Him. Of course that wasn't true, but that is how I related to Him.

We need to take a look at what the authority figures in our lives have taught us, spoken to us — and then determine how much of our response to that we have projected onto God. It took me a regrettably long time to figure out that the way I saw God was quite similar to how I related to my mother when I was a younger adult.

Then it took more time to change that view to where I finally understood who God is and how He operates. One of my favorite verses about God describes Him as *The Lord, the Lord, compassionate and gracious, slow to anger, abounding in love and faithfulness.*[27] And one of my favorite verses about what He does: *We throw open our doors to God and discover at the same moment that he has already thrown open his door to us. We find ourselves standing where we always hoped we might stand – out in the wide open spaces of God's grace and glory, standing tall and shouting our praises.*[28]

---

[27] Exodus 34:6
[28] Romans 5:2 (The Message)

I learned that I didn't need to be afraid of getting it wrong because His nature is love, grace, and forgiveness. When I was seeing things more clearly, it was obvious that God had always been actively at work in my life, directing, providing for me, and healing my wounded heart. That was a message that I needed to hear and receive!

One of the best means we can use to get our thinking about God straightened out is by reading scripture. In the *Appendix: About God*, I list scriptures about who God is. I needed to do that for myself. I did a Bible study for several months, simply looking for details about Him, descriptions of who He is and how He acts. I read these over and over to get it into my thinking, into my heart. He wasn't the APITS (**A**ngry **P**arent **i**n **t**he **S**ky). I was dealing with a God who is amazing. Full of love. The Lord of the *Missio Dei*.

God's heavenly buglight

Larry had a horrible childhood that was quite destructive, full of painful events and relationships. As a result, as an adult, Larry had a lot of issues he struggled against. Thoughts would come unbidden into his mind, thoughts that came because of his brokenness and issues. He didn't want them, hated them, but he couldn't seem to get rid of them. His counselor told Larry that there was a difference between the thoughts coming to him—and Larry embracing and entertaining them. As humans we are thinking all the time. About all kinds of things. Often, we don't pay attention to what we think. Or we don't believe that we have any control over our thinking.

These broken thoughts came to Larry (or they come to us) because they arose out of the damage within him, and from the enemy of his soul, and from the darkness in the world around him, including the people who had spoken abusively to him in the past. He couldn't always control that his mind was harassed in this way. Fact is, this struggle is "natural" for those of us who live in this broken world. But

Larry could certainly control whether he entertained, accepted, and repeated what came into his mind.

This was news to Larry. He had never considered that there were two separate events: the thoughts coming, followed by a second step of believing and accepting the thoughts. So he went home, reflected, and prayed. He definitely *did not* want to continue being tormented. As he prayed, he got a picture of a big buglight (one of those purple UV lights that attract insects and then electrocutes them) in the sky. God's heavenly buglight. Every time one of those negative thoughts came, instead of entertaining it or receiving it, he cast it up into the buglight where it fried with a satisfying *phissst*!

For a while, the unwanted thoughts kept coming. But the good news is that the more we heal, the less those unwanted thoughts come. Sometimes a 100 times a day Larry threw them into the buglight. He didn't entertain them. He continued to work on getting healed from his issues. Eventually, he healed enough that the thoughts didn't come anymore.

We have that same ability. The thoughts may come, but we can make the choice not to entertain them. If we have been saying negative things to ourselves, "I hate how I look." "No one likes having me around." "I am such a loser." That is FOWL language that must stop!

It is a huge step to stop saying those negative words. But things really improve when we *replace* the negative words with positive words. We need to start saying to ourselves and about ourselves words that are true, positive, and uplifting. "I am a woman of value and worth." "I have a lot to contribute." "God gives me grace and beauty." A way to speak true, positive, uplifting words to ourselves is by declaring affirmations.

If you just rolled your eyes and were tempted to stop reading here because the notion of affirmations seems silly, give me a moment to make a case. Affirmations are simply being intentional about saying the right kind of things to ourselves, replacing the old, terrible, negative messages with those that are true, positive, hopeful, and visionary. (You can download a free, helpful worksheet on constructing and using affirmations from my website at artofthriving.net.)

It's all in our heads

It is possible that we may have health, disability, or energy issues that prevent us from doing everything we want to do. But our biggest blockage is most likely in our minds. There could be things we've been thinking that are keeping us stuck. "I'm too old." "No one cares what I have to offer." "I've never done anything like that before." "I tried to do something and it didn't work." "I've got too many physical limitations." Before anything else, we need to try to reverse that thinking.

Too old. Our majority culture does not value the wisdom of the elders. But that doesn't mean we elders need to tuck our tail between our legs and run and hide! In so many ways, we are only as old as we think we are. And who decided how old is "too old," anyway? Age might change the nature and quantity of our contribution, but instead of stopping it, it could make it richer, deeper, and more substantive.

No one wants me. Wrong! If we feel unwanted, we can try making a contribution somewhere. There are many needs that we can fill. We can love an unloved one. There isn't anyone on earth who doesn't need to be loved. We can pray. There is never too much prayer going up for issues and needs. What each of us can offer is needed somewhere. If we believe that and look for an opportunity — asking God to guide us — we *will* find a place to contribute.

Never done it before. And? So what! Can't we learn how now? We need to be bold. If it needs to be done — then we need to try to do it. There is likely someone somewhere who has already done it from whom we could learn. Take it in small steps. Make progress, not perfection.

It didn't work. What does that even mean? Did we have unrealistic expectations that we didn't meet? Did we try once, didn't succeed, and never tried again? Most anything worthwhile is going to take time to figure out, learn, and develop. It's okay to "fail forward." We just need to pick ourselves up, dust ourselves off, and take the next step.

I've got too many physical limitations. There are always going to be limitations and hindrances to anything meaningful and important. But they don't have to stop us. We can work to overcome them. (Or go around them.) From disability services to creative problem solving—there are ways to accomplish what we truly want and intend to accomplish.

I urge you to make a conscious effort to change your FOWL language. Start declaring affirmations today. See what an amazing change it begins to make in all sorts of things—from your attitudes to your sense of possibilities.

Along with changing your FOWL Language, take a look at changing your negative actions.

7: FOWL DEEDS

People pleasing is deadly. Ultimately, it is not even possible.

A juggling act

I was powerfully driven to please people for much of my early, young adult life. It started in my childhood living with a sometimes angry, controlling, and unpredictable mother.[29] People have different responses to that kind of parent. Some become rebellious and disobey in every way that they can. Others shut down. I always tried to be a Good Girl. Tried to make and keep my mom happy. Of course that behavior continued after I left home. I was constantly focused on keeping everyone happy. The only way I could even attempt to keep everyone happy was by suppressing my own preferences and dreams.

One day I had a wakeup call. In my various positions as pastor, I was paid for 40 hours a week, but always worked far more than that, even up to 60 hours. Every elected board member in the church saw themselves as my direct boss—all seven of them! I was constantly trying to keep them happy, but each of them had strongly held—and

---

[29] To be fair, my mother was also loving, took good care of us and the home, had a good sense of humor, and was highly creative and intelligent. Being angry wasn't her only defining characteristic.

quite different—opinions of what needed to happen. Talk about an impossible assignment!

In addition, other people in the church would periodically berate me for not doing what they perceived I should be doing. It was so frustrating, because church members really have *no* idea what is involved in a pastor's daily schedule. Nor do they typically see the bigger picture. But they most definitely have opinions of what should be happening, and how it should be done—and many of these opinions concerned the pastor's job. (Because, don't you know, the pastor is supposed to be doing everything, fixing everything, bringing in all kinds of new people—without causing any change or upsetting any of the people already attending.)

I had a propitious conversation with an elder statesman who had been a pastor for a long time. He was very well respected and a strong leader. In a conversation with him about the struggles I was having with the people in my church, I suddenly realized that, more often than not, as a pastor, I had been diffident, apologetic, and a people pleaser.

This shocked me. Until then, I had not seen that about myself. Being a Good Girl in that position wasn't leadership, especially considering the transformational work that God had given me to do in this assignment. If I was lacking in confidence, apologetic, and a trying to keep everyone happy, I wasn't going to get that work done. If I was allowing myself to be pulled in different directions, I wasn't doing the will of God!

It made a real difference in my leadership once I recognized that and began to make changes in how I operated. I didn't want to go back to being a Good Girl. I didn't want to be that kind of leader. Because that isn't getting God's will done.

Pleasing to death

People pleasing is deadly to our hearts, our dreams, to our lives. If we are always pleasing people, we are not being ourselves, nor fulfilling our call, nor pursuing our dreams, nor obeying God.

Because it is so harmful to be a people pleaser, we must stop. The biggest goal worth pursuing in anyone's life is to please God. And pleasing Him isn't as hard as we might think.[30] Because He loves us like a father. He delights in our obedience, in our love of Him, in our efforts to follow His guidance. And we are not on our own. He is always willing and able to help us to know and do His will.[31]

So we must stop people-pleasing and start to pursue the dreams God has put in our hearts. If we are spending all our time trying to please everyone else, we are not doing what God wants us to do. Often what people want of us will be wrong because they are selfish, confused, lost, broken, or sinful when they ask or demand it. It is so important to be true to ourselves, to who God made each of us to be. We can't do that and be what someone else wants us to be or do.

Besides, if we are trying to please everyone — there are a whole lot of "everyone" out there! What they each want is often going to be in conflict with the other. I remember hearing about a church, one that practiced communion on a regular basis. The church needed new altar cloths. There was a disagreement among the members of the altar guild over *how many stitches per inch* went into the pieces. It ended up splitting the church!

You can't possibly please everyone. Trying to do so only ends up just making a mess of everything.

---

[30] Matthew 11:30
[31] Philippians 2:13

The "good" disease

I was certainly a committed Good Girl for much of my adult life. The odds are, you have also been a Good Girl. The Good Girl Syndrome is a wide-spread disease among women, characterized by not rocking the boat, trying to keep everyone happy, doing what everyone expects of us. However, if we are being a Good Girl, we are probably not being God's Girls.

I urge us to dare to disappoint—everyone except God. If we stop people pleasing, we will inevitably disappoint someone. But we must get off that treadmill of trying to please. It is never ending. People are so often greedy, selfish, desperate, and needy. If they—or we—have designated us to please them, we will never be done.

We need, instead, to turn to God and say, *You alone are the One I want to please. You alone know what the right thing to do is. You know what you made me to be and do; how You mean me to live in this life. I don't want anything else except You and what You want. Help me offload the expectations of everyone else. I just want to do what You put in front of me to do.*

Don't be a Good Girl. *Do* Good, girl!

8: FOWL WEATHER

If you are in a relationship where you are always watching the emotional weather, something needs to change.

Call it what it is

As I mentioned previously, I was raised in a home with an angry mom. She would become outraged at something one of us kids did, screaming angrily one time, but then, at another time, she wouldn't even notice. Her anger was unpredictable. So I was always tiptoeing around. Always very alert to the emotional weather so I would know if I was in danger of getting yelled at, of making her mad.

That was abusive. If we are in a relationship that is abusive, that needs to stop. If we are having to watch the emotional weather with someone, be on guard against making them angry, always alert for someone's out-of-control anger, watching for the fist to come swinging—that must stop. We need to end the abuse. Abuse destroys. It is time to say, "This far and no further."

Victim and bully

My response to that abuse turned me into a victim. Because I had learned victimization well, after leaving home, I continued to be a victim of abusers for much of my adult life, always being hurt by what people said and did to me—and then wondering what I had done wrong to cause it. Wondering why they would be so mean to me, especially since I meant well and tried so hard.

One day, as I was reflecting on this issue, I realized that there had never been a time in my life when I did not have someone attacking me, never a time, in any place I lived, where I didn't have my own "personal" abuser. I remembered when I was in graduate school. There were two women in particular who were so mean and awful to me. They said derogatory things to me in class, they made disparaging comments about me to others. I reminded my husband about that situation, and his take on it was, "They were bullies." That word opened up my thinking. There was never a time in my life when I didn't have a bully oppressing me!

Pairings and patterns

I realized that the victim in me somehow attracted the abuser in others. When we see a repeated pattern like that occurring in our life, we need to look at *ourselves*. There is something within us that is contributing to that pattern in our life.

There are many kinds of brokenness that pair up with other brokenness. Abusers and predators seek out victims, the indecisive attracts dominators, manipulators are attracted to the weak. Whatever the issue, the pattern is almost always unconscious until we see it and begin to recognize it in our life.

This too

A part of any woman's journey to maturity in her walk of faith as a Christ follower must include the journey toward emotional wholeness. We need to examine any area of our life that is not thriving and look more deeply than we have before. God and I worked on changing my victim mentality over a period of several years. I am thankful that God ended that pattern of thinking in my life. I have been healed and being a victim no longer characterizes my life.

If you are being abused, look for help. None of us are meant to stand alone. You—and all of us—are always meant to be part of the community of God. This is especially true of the person who is wounded and vulnerable. We can't get free of abuse or any brokenness by ourselves. We need people to stand with us, to help us be strong while we are learning to be strong.

But we must stop being a victim of abuse. We need to regain our power. Come in out of the FOWL weather.

.

As mentioned previously, you can download a free overview of the inner healing process at my website.

I also go into much greater detail about inner healing in my book *The Art of Thriving: 12 Life Skills for Living Well.*

If you want to know more about the ministry of transforming prayer, mentioned in *Core Principle: Healing the Wounded Heart,* go to my website artofthriving.net. Look for the Grace Abounds Ministries page.

9: CUTE CHICK

Our society worships at the altar of youth and beauty. Our society is nuts. You know that you have far more value than just your age and looks, right?

Impossible attainment

Men have always liked a good looking woman, but it truly seems like our current culture has toppled over the edge with the pursuit and idolization of youth and beauty. In an effort to be honest, I concede that it might be more apparent to me because I am older, and youth and what beauty I ever had are far behind me, but I don't think that's the whole reason. In a culture where everything from cars to toothpaste is sold by sex, where every week there is a new, impossibly beautiful (and impossibly skinny) singer or actress hitting the gossip rags, where "Does she or doesn't she?" most often refers to whether she has had plastic surgery—it is crazy-hard to be satisfied with what you look like, what you weigh, and how old you are.

Miss-focused

In North America, beauty is a multi-billion-dollar industry. Cosmetics, clothing, and fashion. The fitness industry. The print publication industry *about* fashion and cosmetics. If you think about it, it is simply astounding. All that time, attention, effort, and money spent on appearance, on reversing aging, fixing flaws, improving the appearance of our physical body. Which is, no matter how hard we try, still unavoidably heading toward the grave! Ya gotta ask: Is it appropriate to be spending that kind of money, time, and effort on something that is so ultimately inconsequential and transient?

The challenges of FOWL

I admit that I am weight "challenged." I am heavier than I should be, heavier than I want to be. (And with menopause, dadgummit if it hasn't become harder and harder to do anything about that!) According to our culture's standards, I am chronologically challenged (as in, "old"). I am gender challenged (being female). I am appearance challenged (being not beautiful).

Never mind that I have intelligence, high energy, talents, deep creativity, competence, an entrepreneurial, innovative mind, a Type-A personality. I am housed in an aging, overweight, female body. People see my outside far more often than they see what's inside.

You may have experienced similar blindness in your place of work or service. Beautiful young women, in general, experience far more open doors than "average"-looking, older, and/or overweight women.

Our culture has also decided that seniority is useless, even embarrassing; that the opinions of youth matter more than those of maturity. Simple experience tells you how ridiculous that is, yet the trend toward listening to and considering only the opinions of youth persists. Our culture has also decreed that we have an expiration date. After a certain age, the opinion goes, we can no longer contribute, so we are free to "retire." We not only can but should back off, leave it to younger others.

True worth

In our society, being a FOWL feels like a death sentence; or, at the very least, sentenced to irrelevance. The older we are, the less others think we know. Physical limitations are assumed to demonstrate equivalent mental deterioration. Add in a lack of interest in or facility with the latest in technology—and we are looked at as ready for the dumpster in the alley!

Thankfully, that is so far from being necessary, appropriate, or even practical! The world may not know how ridiculous it is, but we need to. Why should a faceless "them" get to decide when we are done, or if we will be permitted to continue to contribute? Our so-called "twilight" time of life could be as productive as any that went before!

It really doesn't matter how others (who are ignorant) see us. Physical beauty is only superficial and youth passes (oh so quickly!) away. But who we are—our character, our intelligence, our depth of experience, our maturity—remains, and only becomes richer with time and attention. We have strong and well-tested relational skills. We have stamina and perseverance. Many of us have a deep spirituality.

Anyone with any sense knows that these are far more valuable than something so ephemeral as youth and beauty. Why can't our "golden years" be truly *golden*—rich, full, fabulous, and valuable? This is certainly how things work in the Kingdom of God—and, really, what else matters?

All that being said—and being true—it is remarkably hard to disengage from the value measurements of our culture to accept ourselves as having worth apart from our looks and weight; to accept that we have something to offer other than our appearance and sex appeal.

Our culture has got it completely wrong. It is very easy to just go with the flow, get sucked into the lie. Even when it is bad for us. But it is. Bad for us.

The answer isn't belligerence or anger. We need to forgive. But we also need to go ahead and do the next right thing. No hostility. Operate in wisdom and love. But move forward.

It takes a determined effort to wrench our focus away *from* all of that and *to* the important and eternal. But there *is* something far more eternal and important! Realizing that God loves you, that He is personally and deeply interested in you, that He treasures you[32] and wants to hold you close to His heart,[33] to protect you under the shadow of His wings[34] — can help you make that shift. Our identity in Christ — as beloved daughters,[35] bought with a price,[36] and precious to our Heavenly Father — gives us our value, not our age and looks.

In the next chapter we talk about a truly appropriate focus.

---

[32] Psalm 18:19
[33] Isaiah 40:11
[34] Psalm 36:7
[35] Galatians 4:6
[36] 1 Corinthians 6:20

10: FOWL THINGS UP

Whatever you are worshipping that isn't God needs to be dropped like a hot potato. Stop worshipping any lesser thing and give your worship to the One it rightly belongs to—God, and God alone.

What do you love?

Okay, did that shock you? You, a good Christian woman, worshipping something other than God? Never!

But don't be so hasty. By worship, I am talking about being absorbed by something, deeply engrossed by the details, much of your time consumed by it, can't get enough of it, living vicariously through it, spending money on it, treasuring, even coddling and petting it, looking for meaning by being involved in it.

By that definition, our culture today worships at the altars of many idols. Money. Youth. Sex.

Have you observed how our culture worships celebrity? Weekly fan magazines, websites, Twitter feeds are devoted to reporting in tiny detail the lives of the rich and famous. When a celebrity promotes a product, masses of people buy the product. When one simply wears a particular item, that item sells off the shelves in a matter of days or hours. Movie stars testify before our government on different policy and budget issues. We are so enamored by celebrity that there are now people who are famous simply for being famous!

Millions of people spend their lives living vicariously through the lives of the people they watch in a seemingly infinite number of reality shows because it is escapism—and our culture worships escapism. Some of the highest paid people in our country have a job throwing a ball back and forth because we idolize sports and the people who play them. Billions of dollars are spent on makeup every year because we've made an idol of beauty, and on skin care products because we've made an idol of youth. Unbelievable amounts of money are spent on the latest new tech gadget, music downloads, video games, and movies, because we worship entertainment.

A certain fan magazine nearly always has a section on a celebrity's house being sold for some multi-millions of dollars. We are shown shots of the interior. Why does one couple need a house with 12 bathrooms and 10 bedrooms, and 4 sitting rooms? Or gold-gilded doorways? Or a fully-equipped personal movie studio? Only because we have made an idol of conspicuous consumption. If someone makes it financially, the first thing they do is buy a fancy car and a big house, and start walking around with arm candy.

Our culture has a great many gods!

A dead end

However, only Almighty God, Lord of the Angel Armies, is worthy of worship. Everything else is empty; a dead end. And it really irritates God. I love this passage in Isaiah where God is describing to His foolish people exactly what they are doing when they worship an idol that they have made with their own hands. *Half of the wood he burns in the fire; over it he prepares his meal, he roasts his meat and eats his fill. He also warms himself and says, "Ah! I am warm; I see the fire." From the rest he makes a god, his idol; he bows down to it and worships. He prays to it and says, "Save me! You are my god!"*[37] From the same wood that he uses to bake his food and warm himself, he carves an idol with his own hands that he then bows down and worships as his god, expecting this god to save him! When you think about it this way, worshipping as god something that is human or human made is profoundly… silly!

Yet that is what we are doing when we think about a celebrity in the way I described as worship: when we follow their every word, fashion style, and details of their dating life. When we are absorbed by studying them and imitating them, much of our time consumed by following them on social media. When we can't get enough of learning everything about them, looking at pictures of them, reading about their life. When we live vicariously through their life, when we spend money on the pursuit of ever more detail about them, when we find meaning by being involved in following, discussing, tracking them with other fans.

The thing is, celebrities are just people. Not much different from us. Worse, many of them are not admirable; they don't live an honorable, noble life. They are famous and happen to be good looking. But very few of them are decent role models.

But it does demonstrate that our hearts want to worship. They need to. If we don't worship God, then we'll worship something—and that something will be far less worthy.

Fine tuning

Our hearts are like a satellite dish. For good reception, in order to get the signal that you want, sometimes you need to refocus the dish back onto the satellite because it has gotten blown or knocked out of alignment. The satellite dish of our hearts needs to be focused on God. Our Creator, who desires to have a relationship of love with us, is

---

[37] Isaiah 44:15-17

who our hearts were designed for. Anything else will not satisfy. This means that sometimes we need to realign our hearts back on God. If we have FOWLed things up by focusing on and worshipping the wrong thing, we need to get untangled and get realigned.

One important tool for fine tuning the satellite dish is having a regular time spent with the Lord. Most people prefer to do this first thing in the morning, before the day starts, but that isn't a rule. Such a set-aside time could include reading the Word of God and reflecting on it, prayer (including praise, supplication, repentance, and intercession), and reading a daily devotional and reflecting on that. Having an expectation that God will speak to you is important. When He does, your heart is refreshed, your attitudes recalibrated, and your focus realigned.

Following Christ and belonging to God should change us. Are we different because we seek and obey God? If we are just going through the religious motions, all we'll find is emptiness. But if the pursuit of God engages our passion, our love, and our hope, then we will find greater fulfillment than we ever thought possible.

If you want a little worksheet for how to have a quiet time, you can download it free at my website artofthriving.net.

Guard the gate

We need to protect our hearts; be very careful what we are pursuing, where we focus our passion, our desire, our imitation, our energy. We must not let in stuff that doesn't belong. We need to protect our hearts from being ravaged by something that is unworthy.[38]

I love a good story and have TV shows I like to follow. However, one day I sort of woke up and realized that the show I had been watching had repeated acts of violence. And I felt a check in my spirit: did I want to be allowing that stuff to come into my heart and mind?

---

[38] Proverbs 4:23

No, I did not! Since that time, I started being far more careful and selective about TV, movies, books. If we don't guard our hearts, who will?

Following a false trail

The world around us is pursuing things that don't satisfy. No one seems to know what they are actually searching for. Without focus or purpose, our lives feel empty. Then, to fill the emptiness, our response is often to do more activity and to consume more, hoping the increased volume will fill us up. Yet, consuming more and more is still worthless and still leaves us feeling empty. More of whatever it is still doesn't make *enough* — not if it isn't the right thing. The right response, instead — like when we take a wrong turn and the GPS says, "Recalculating" — is to back off, take a deep breath, and redirect. Make a U-turn.

The only one worthy of the worship of our heart is God. Is your heart hungry for something else? It is misguided. The truth is, our hearts were made for God alone. We will not be satisfied without Him. *Thou hast made us for Thyself, O Lord, and our heart is restless until it finds its rest in Thee.*[39] We're made to find our true self and our right path in Him. *In Him we live and move and have our being.*[40]

What are you focusing on? Where are you putting your attention? If not on God, it is not on the right thing. I urge you to realign.

---

[39] St. Augustine
[40] Acts 27:28

Fat Old White Lady

W.E.I.T.

It can feel intimidating, scary, or even boring to think about working to get healed, to clean up the rubble in our lives. But healing is essential if we are going to live a good life and if we are going to make a significant contribution to the world around us. Our damage will prevent both. So we need to decide to do <u>W</u>hat <u>E</u>ver <u>I</u>t <u>T</u>akes so that we can be useful, so that we can contribute meaningfully and significantly. We need to commit to letting God have at us, responding in obedience and trust, surrendering ourselves into His good care.

Fat Old White Lady

SECTION TWO WORKBOOK

Core Principle: Healing the Wounded Heart

1. Do you recognize that you have behaviors or attitudes that need to be changed? Do you need to make a U-turn? What would that look like? Make a plan for a needed U-turn in your life. What will you do differently?

2. Had you ever before considered that Jesus had a "mission statement"? Take a look at each of the items listed in His declaration (Luke 4:18) and the longer, more complete passage from which Jesus quotes (Isaiah 61:1-5). Where in His life (as described in the Gospels) did you see Him fulfilling these passages? Where has He carried out His mission in *your* life?

3. What do you think of the idea that Jesus' mission includes healing the brokenhearted? Does it give you inspiration to let God deal with your own wounded heart? Are you able to accept the idea that your heart *could* be healed? That God not only wants that for you, He is eager to help you have it? Will you let Him start today?

4. Have you worked these steps for healing your wounded heart?
   - ❏ Acknowledge the pain
   - ❏ Decide that you want to be healed
   - ❏ Enter the process of healing

   What could you do to take a step in that direction? If you haven't yet done so, read my road map for healing the wounded heart. (Download from the website or find ordering directions in the back pages of this book.)

5. Do you take God seriously? Do you know who He is? Do you know what He asks of you? Is direct and specific obedience even on your grid? Take some time to pray and journal about where you stand with God. What, if anything, needs to change?

6. If you have not done so, could you avail yourself of any of these tools for being healed?
   - ❏ Resources. (Teachings, books, professionals)
   - ❏ Journaling.
   - ❏ Counseling.
   - ❏ Support groups.
   - ❏ Community.

FOWL Yourself

7. In your journal, diagram what self-care you are doing in each area of your life: spiritual, physical/health, mental. Is your current level of self-care adequate? Are you caring properly for every area? Are you eating healthy? Getting enough sleep? Getting enough socialization? Enough mental stimulation? Enough time with God? If not, determine what you should change. Set small goals for improvement in two or three areas. Once you've reached and are sustaining those goals, create new ones.

8. What do you think of the concept that the highest in the human hierarchy (body, soul, and spirit) is not body nor mind, but spirit? If that is true, do you need to make some changes in how you approach your life?

9. This chapter made the claim that the journey toward maturity includes appropriate self-care and healing. Do you agree? Is it possible to be spiritually mature and still be unhealed? Have you worked on this in your own life?

FOWL Language

10. Have you had experiences where someone said negative, hurtful things to you? (Things like, "You are so stupid." "You'll never amount to anything." "You're ugly. No man will want you.") What did they say? How did it affect you? (Did it make you feel stupid? Or worthless? Like you could never achieve anything? Unwanted, unloved?) Are you still dealing with that effect? Did you start saying those negative

things to yourself? Believing them and acting on them? Take time to reflect in your journal on some of the powerful words that have been spoken to you and their impact on your life.

11. Has your view of or opinion about God been affected or altered by something negative said or done to you? Have you, like I did, transferred your perceptions and attitudes about an authority figure onto God? Do you now need to make some adjustments?

12. Is the idea of God's Big Buglight in the Sky helpful to you? Would it work to help you get rid of the negative thoughts that invade your mind?

13. Did this chapter get you thinking about using affirmations? Have you tried them before? Why or why not? Consider downloading the step-by-step worksheet for crafting and using affirmations from the artofthriving.net website.

14. Have you said and believed any of the reasons at the end of the chapter for not doing anything?

    ❑ I'm too old.
    ❑ No one wants me.
    ❑ I've never done anything like that before.
    ❑ I tried to do something and it didn't work.
    ❑ I have too many limitations.

    What do you think now? Can you reconsider your stance?

15. Have you looked at the scriptures in the *Appendix: About Us* that talk about how God sees you? If not, take some time right now to do so. How do they affect you? How is your sense of self shifting as you read them?

FOWL Deeds

16. Are you infected with the Good Girl Syndrome? Do you see yourself characterized by not rocking the boat, keeping everyone happy, doing what everyone expects of you? How is that working for you?

17. Do you work to inappropriately please someone(s) in your life? What does that look like? Looking as objectively as you can, is your people pleasing healthy? What does it do to that relationship? (Is it an honest relationship? Is it unequal? For example, one person doing all the giving and the other all the taking?) What would the relationship be like if you stopped people pleasing? Can you begin to make some changes?

18. What do you think of the challenge to "dare to disappoint everyone except God"? Could you take that dare? How does the idea make you feel? (Anxious? Sick? Relieved?)

19. If you have recognized that you are a people pleaser, what does people pleasing do to you? How does it affect your own sense of self-worth? Your ability to follow your dreams? Do the will of God? Begin to journal on these questions. Take a deep look at what is most important for you at this time in your life.

20. Are you able to pray the prayer that ended the *FOWL Deeds*?

> *You alone are the One I want to please. You alone know what the right thing to do is. You know what you made me to be and do; how You mean me to live in this life. I don't want anything else except You and what You want. Help me off-load the expectations of everyone else. I just want to do what You put in front of me to do.*

FOWL Weather

21. Do you have a relationship in which you are watching the emotional "weather"? Have you talked to someone outside of that situation, someone safe, about it yet? Why not? If you have not begun to address it, start today. It's important.

22. Do you have a negative, destructive pattern evident in your life? For instance, do you have a relationship that regularly gets uncomfortable? Do you keep ending up doing an activity that you dislike because you feel pressured into it? Do you often feel afraid of that other person? Can you see a way in which your brokenness works in an unhealthy way with that

Section Two Workbook

of someone else—like the example in the chapter (predator and victim, manipulator and weak, etc.)? Takes steps today to begin to change that. Start by looking for help, someone to walk with you through the process of getting healthy. Start journaling about this relationship, how it got started, how you came to cooperate with this pattern of relating.

23. What did you think of this statement: "A part of any woman's journey to maturity in her walk of faith as a Christ follower must include the journey toward emotional wholeness"? Do you agree? Disagree? Why? Have you made pursuing emotional wholeness part of your journey?

FOWL Smell

24. Did this chapter cause you to recognize that you have some untreated garbage in the basement of your soul that needs to be dealt with? Do you live with self-hate or some other form of negative, destructive attitudes toward yourself? Do you have hurt deep in your soul from something that happened or something that was said to you? Do you want to be healed? If you want to pursue healing, download my "road map" for inner healing from artofthriving.net website and get started.

25. To begin to practice self-appreciation where you haven't been appreciative, try adding to an on-going self-appreciation list every day. In your journal, make a list of the things you did, the words you spoke, the thoughts you had that you feel were good, worthwhile, and worthy of appreciation. Try to come up with a minimum of three items each day. Try this exercise for a period of time (2-3 months) so that it actually has time to work on the way that you think about yourself. The goal isn't to get an inflated sense of self. The goal is to change the negative, awful, derogatory feelings you currently have about yourself. To recognize your worth and value.

Cute Chick

26. Have you ever felt that you've been given an "expiration date" because of your age? That you were discarded because of your age or looks? Or made to feel irrelevant?

27. Have you personally experienced the preferential treatment that beautiful and young women tend to receive (either as one or seeing it happen to another)? Has that preference impacted you personally? How so?

28. Have you bought our culture's "company line" that you are too old, too fat, too female to be useful? After reading this chapter, are you willing to let go of that lie? Can you allow yourself to see your worth and value apart from your appearance? Do you believe that you still have something to contribute? Start thinking about what that is and what you could do to offer it.

29. Have you examined the amount of money, time, and effort you spend on beauty? Is it appropriate, healthy, or morally right? Do you need to make any changes?

FOWL Things Up

30. Do you have a quiet time with the Lord? If not, why not? Would you consider starting one now?

31. Is the satellite dish of your heart in need of some realignment? Reading the chapter, did you discover that you might be guilty of worshipping something other than God? Do you have a focus (maybe even an obsession) on something that truthfully isn't worth that time and attention? Could you make the shift in your attention to something far more worthwhile? What would that pursuit be?

32. Have you found that being in relationship with God, following the Lord Christ has changed you? In what ways? If not, why not?

33. Go through the footnoted scriptures. Look at them in the context used in this book. What did you learn? Did you change an opinion? Will you now change an action?

SECTION THREE: GROWTH

There is a progression to our life in God. In the previous section, we looked at the importance of engaging in repair work. Dealing with the damage in our souls, cleaning up the rubble in our lives. In Section Three, we look at our next step: growth.

Fat Old White Lady

CORE PRINCIPLE: TREASURES OF DARKNESS

We go through hard things. What makes all the difference is how we respond to those difficult events.

It's all in the response

Bad things happen. And they happen to good people. That is a consequence of living in a broken, sinful world. None of us are exempt from the hard things. So what do we do about it? How do we handle it? How do we understand or find meaning in the middle of it?

In my young adult years, I had a very difficult encounter with a significant person in my life. She said things that were full of vitriol, and said them in such a way as to cause me the most hurt possible. It was a deeply painful event that left me shattered. As a result, among other issues, I developed PTSD.[41]

I suffered from it for a long time without realizing that PTSD was what I struggled with. But, as PTSD does, it affected nearly every area of my life. I felt like a victim, out of control of the events of my life, helpless, full of shame and self-blame, distrusting of others.

---

[41] Post-Traumatic Stress Disorder. A mental health problem that can occur after a person goes through a traumatic event (like war, an assault, or an accident).

I struggled to find a way forward. I did work on my issues. I experienced healing in many ways. But there was stuff that persisted, no matter how hard I tried.

One day, God simply spoke into my thoughts. I clearly heard the Holy Spirit tell me that that terrible event caused me to develop PTSD. (Before that moment, that idea had not been on my mind at all!)

At that point I only knew of PTSD. I knew that it was not uncommon for soldiers who had seen battle to develop PTSD, causing them all sorts of difficulties when they tried to assimilate back into civilian life.

Immediately, I went online to study this disorder. I saw what I had been disabled with laid out there right before me! That day, I learned something else that made all the difference. Researchers found that when the same traumatic event happens to two people, one can move on and eventually be fine, but the other falls apart. What makes the biggest difference? How the sufferer responds. In other words, it wasn't the event that ultimately mattered. It was the individual's response to the event.

I also learned that the way forward from PTSD was to overcome the sense of helplessness, learn strategies and coping skills, reclaim my sense of power, and take positive action.

It was encouraging to realize that I had already been doing some of that for some time. It was empowering to me to realize that the biggest part of moving forward in a positive way from something that was traumatic is under my control!

There is a relatively new field of study in psychology called Post-Traumatic Growth (PGT).[42] This is recognizing that some people do more than simply rebound; display more than resilience after a traumatic event. They actually grow. They come out changed—for the

---

[42] www.ptgi.uncc.edu/what-is-ptg

better. Stronger, more positive and hopeful, more focused (actually, re-focused) on making more of their life.

We may not be able to control what happens to us. We may not have control over other people, circumstances, or things. But we do have control over our own attitude, over our own choices, over our own responses.

It's your choice

There are at least four things that we can do to respond to difficulties in a positive, life-affirming, hopeful way:

Make the decision to keep positive. Look for the good. Press forward with hope. It doesn't necessarily make the consequences easier, but it makes surviving them and moving beyond them toward something better more possible. Our attitude is under our control if we choose to exercise that control.

Maintain integrity. In the face of hard things, unpleasant things, there is the temptation to behave badly: to lose our temper, to whine and complain, to give tit for tat, to burn bridges. But we can also choose to keep doing the right thing, to refrain from doing something that we will regret later.

Persevere. Few things, including hardships, last forever. Persevering — continuing to hang in there, keeping our attitude positive, handling things rightly — takes strength of character... and builds strength of character.[43]

Surrender the situation and ourselves to God. Paul is really clear, when he writes about perseverance and suffering, that God uses these things in our lives for good.[44] God doesn't necessarily *bring* them, but He *uses* everything. If we will let Him, He will use these hard things in our lives to make us the people He always meant us to be. And to

---

[43] Romans 5:3-5; James 1:2-4
[44] Romans 8:28

prepare us for the works of service He has planned for us to do.[45]

Although God is always at work in our lives, He will not violate our free will, so we can actually limit the work God does in us. But if we yield ourselves to Him and permit Him, He works deeply, actively, and continuously. It is up to us to choose how we will respond. We can allow the hard things we go through, the things that happened in the darkness of pain, to turn into treasures — treasures born of darkness.[46]

The Joseph story

Because I have been through more than one fiery trial, the story of Joseph has ministered to me for several years.[47] As a youth, he was given a prophetic word through a vision — twice (giving double confirmation) — that God would put him into a position of prominence to such a degree that his father and brothers would bow down to him.

At the time Joseph received those visions from God, he was shallow, spoiled, immature, and arrogant. God had to deal with him, and it wasn't pretty. First, his brothers captured Joseph, and he heard them discussing how they would kill him. In the end, they didn't kill him, but they did sell him into slavery in Egypt, far from home. There, in the home of his master, Joseph is eventually put in charge of the household, and everything he does prospers. But then he is falsely accused of rape by his master's wife and ends up thrown in prison. Once again, Joseph is put in charge of the prisoners and everything he does prospers.

One day, two fellow prisoners, who had been in the service of the pharaoh, but had displeased him and had been thrown in prison, have dreams and Joseph is able to interpret them. One man hears the

---

[45] Ephesians 2:10
[46] Isaiah 45:3
[47] Genesis 37 - 47

good news that he will be restored to the service of the pharaoh. Joseph asks that man to remember him when he gets out. The man does get out, just as Joseph had prophesied, but he forgets what he promised, and Joseph languishes in prison for another two years.

But then, after all that time, Joseph gets a "suddenly"—a moment when it all came together; when everything that God had been doing in him, around him, and through him reached its fulfillment. The pharaoh has a dream that he knows is significant, and when no one among his advisors can interpret it, the man who had been in prison finally remembers Joseph's astoundingly accurate ability to interpret dreams. Joseph is brought before Pharaoh to interpret Pharaoh's dream—which he does. He also tosses in some solid advice about how to handle the problem that the dream revealed—a severe famine to come in the near future. The Pharaoh takes that advice to heart, and then promotes Joseph so that he can deal with the upcoming famine. There, in one moment, Joseph is made the second most powerful man in the world, second only to Pharaoh. He moves from pit, to prison, to palace, to prime minister! God did this so that Joseph was in position to preserve God's people when a terrible famine develops.

The Joseph journey

We see in Joseph's story the way God deals with the people He calls to serve Him. Three things happened to and in Joseph from what he went through:

- *Refined.* The experiences refined his character. He had some serious character flaws and his experiences burned those out of him.
- *Trained.* He was put into positions of progressively increasing responsibility where his natural gift of administration, organizing, and leadership was developed. He gained lots of on-the-job experience (the best kind).

- *Positioned*. He was in the right place at the right time to be put into an crucial position of influence and power. At only age 30, he is promoted to Pharaoh's right hand.

God does the same thing with us. He cleans us up, deals with our sin. He trains us in our gifts. Then He positions us for effectiveness in service. We usually find parts of this process as unpleasant as Joseph did. But the fulfillment of being in a place where, using our gifts and skills, we are able to serve effectively and make a real difference, makes it worth all that we went through to get there.

Again, our choice

The thing to note is that, during all these hardships, Joseph remained faithful to God. We can see that throughout the story. For one thing, the Holy Spirit was still speaking through him because he was still interpreting dreams.[48] We read that Joseph names his sons in a way that demonstrates he still recognizes God at work in his life.[49] When his brothers first come before him, never suspecting that they know him, he does mess with them (a bit cruelly, truth be told). But then he repents and forgives them because he suddenly sees that God had been at work all along. He sees the bigger picture.[50]

Because of Joseph's continued trust in God (even in the face of horrible things like being sold into slavery by his brothers and being falsely accused — and let's not forget those final two years before he is brought before Pharaoh, which must have been the worst of all) he endured the refining (which is never fun), he went through the training and got very good at what he did. He was ready when God positioned him.

Joseph's story is very powerful. We can learn from Joseph to let the trials and suffering make us deeper, more focused on God, more

---

[48] Genesis 40
[49] Genesis 41:50-52
[50] Genesis 45:4-8

responsive, more full of love. We have the choice how we will respond.

The goal of God's work in us is to enable us to remain steady, not easily intimidated when the going gets tough. To make us overcomers.[51] The going *will* get tough. There will always be opposition to God's work in the world. God looks for people who can be trusted to keep going anyway—because there is work to do.

---

[51] Revelations 3:21; Revelations 12:11

Fat Old White Lady

11: FOWL FRITTERS

We need to say no to a wasted life.

Cheap thrills; empty calories

Let's be honest: are we watching too much TV? Indulging in too much gossip? Reading too many trashy romance novels? Spending too much time and money on senior weekend gambling trips? Puttering around aimlessly all day, every day? I see too many of us active seniors active in meaningless pursuits.

My grandmother was a dear lady. I was fortunate to grow up in the same town as her, enjoying her at family dinners and holidays. She was always one of my favorite people.

Jobs moved her adult children away. Fewer and fewer family members were left in town. Grandpa died and then she was alone. She didn't drive, and so relied on two remaining grandchildren to give her an occasional ride, pick up and do her laundry, take her to church. She didn't read much, and the TV was on for most of the day (something to fill the silence).

As a young woman, I felt badly that I couldn't seem to get there more often. I felt very guilty after I moved out of town for work, leaving my sister as her sole relationship and caretaker.

Looking back as an adult, it feels to me like her life consisted of vast tracts of emptiness, with an occasional visit thrown in. Thinking about it now, I can't imagine how lonely she felt, how empty and long were her days. And I wonder why she did that to herself? Did she see no other options?

It is a profound grief to think that women are out there wasting their precious lives, living through days and years empty of any meaning. It is beyond sad to think that so many of us fritter away our lives as if we were marking time, just waiting for death to come knocking on our door.

I know, for some people, the inevitability of death is the *reason* for living life aimlessly. I guess their thinking is: *Eat, drink, and be merry, for tomorrow we die.*[52] In other words, it's all going to end, so why bother doing anything important or meaningful?

But, at least for those of us in Christ, the end of this life is *not* the end! Not at all! There is eternity with our best Friend, with our loving Father, with our Holy Comforter. And life there is a continuing of our life here. We get started now, and continue forever.

Purpose, meaning, and fulfillment

Our lives are a gift from God. Our lives are *not* meaningless. Life is precious. Our lives are precious. What God did through Jesus' death on the Cross ought to prove that. If God thinks you are precious enough to send His Son to die for you, who is going to tell you otherwise?

Many people feel their lives have no purpose. That there is no reason for living. They never consider doing anything significant with their time and energy.

But our lives don't have to feel meaningless. Not if we pursue purpose. **Purpose** is having a goal, something to accomplish.

---

[52] Luke 12:19; 1 Corinthians 15:32

11: FOWL Fritters

Meaning is most often found in making a contribution, making a difference, making the world better, finding that our lives matter.

And using our gifts, expressing our passions and our interests results in personal *fulfillment*.

So we can find fulfillment *and* meaning by using our talents and skills in making a difference somewhere, somehow.

We can do that! In ways big and small. We need to realize just how rich our lives could be! And then we leave a rich legacy behind us. Does it get any better than that?

Fat Old White Lady

12: FOWL AIR

If food sits around without refrigeration, it spoils. You've been in a room that has been shut up for a long time; the air is stale and musty. The same thing happens with us as people. We must always be growing. If we are not attending to our own growth, we get stale, out of date, and disconnected.

It's natural

Virtually everything God made grows until it reaches maturity. This is true in the plant and animal kingdoms. So, too, human beings have physical maturity to achieve. But we are meant to grow in many other areas of our life as well: spiritually, intellectually, emotionally, socially, in the use of our gifts, in our skills, in maturity.[53] In these areas, we need never stop growing. It is part of who we are as creatures made in God's image.[54] We have these incredible brains that are constantly learning and retaining what we learn. We are born with talents that enable us to do certain things well, and are given spiritual gifts that allow us to do ministry empowered by the Holy Spirit. We have so much potential. We should be growing in all these areas. Lack

---
[53] Hebrews 12:14
[54] Genesis 1:27

of intentional growth is lack of self-care.

However, most of us have not come close to reaching our full potential. Our bodies can grow into physical maturity with only the basic maintenance from us (food, sleep, exercise, and other rudimentary self-care). Aging happens without our help. But maturity requires intentionality. Growth of the mind and soul require purposefulness. That is part of what it means to be fully human: to grow into who we were always meant to be.

We can put up barriers to growth. We can decide that we are done, too stupid to learn, or don't have anything to contribute—so why bother. But we can also take those barriers down.

Only cats need worry

Curiosity leads to growth, so developing and indulging a healthy sense of curiosity is a way to keep ourselves fresh. I had a friend whose job was growing less and less satisfying. One day he asked himself the question: How can I become self-supporting in five years? (He was in his mid-30s at the time.) That question opened him up to explore possibilities, to think outside of his box. He discovered options he had never previously considered (like increasing in financial literacy which lead to investing in real estate). He was able to stop working at a job and become self-supporting within *four* years!

Curiosity can lead to asking good questions—questions whose answers change everything. Years ago, I had things I wanted to write, but I could never seem to actually sit down and write them. Something held me back, year after year. Finally, I asked my own right question: Why am I not writing? That led to counseling, which led to profound insight into a whole lot of stuff. And here I am writing!

Training vs. trying hard

I have typically been someone who enjoys getting better at something. A while back, God put His finger on an area of my life that needed improvement, and I was willing to do that work. But it was an area where I had already struggled for years to do better.

I am capable of getting a lot done in a short amount of time. If I focus and crank it up, I am a dynamo, especially when motivated by a deadline. The problem was that, while I was almost always able to find motivation and drive for whatever employment I had, I had a much harder time doing that for myself as a self-employed person. Now that I was actually attempting to be self-employed, I needed to find a way to have a high level of productivity on a regular basis doing my own work. I kept trying to do better, but didn't notice much improvement.

Then I heard a speaker talk about the importance of training. It was a real eye opener. Everyone, no matter the level of their natural gifting, needs to train—and to *practice* that training—in order to achieve true proficiency. From athletes to musicians, from teachers to politicians, everyone benefits from training and practicing in both their skill and gift areas. There is a big difference between trying harder and *training* for improvement.

I needed to apply that principle to several areas of my life—time management, writing, marketing, design. I had never been self-employed before, responsible only to myself. It involved a whole new set of skills—which I needed to develop. So I took classes, looked for and found tools, and worked on incremental improvement.

True maturity

Not only should we be growing and developing our skills, as well as developing as people of good character, but we should also be growing spiritually. The goal of every Christian should be maturity as a Christian. The ultimate definition of maturity is when the nature and character and mind of Christ is formed in us.[55] God is making

---

[55] Galatians 4:19; 1 Corinthians 2:16

us — if we will let Him — into the image of His Son.[56]

One aspect of Christ being formed in us is the giving of spiritual gifts[57] by the Holy Spirit and then our growth in and development of those gifts. No one person gets all the gifts. But each person gets some gifts and then, together, we, as the community, the Body of Christ, display the fullness of Christ (from Whom all the gifts come), and do His work in the world.

A step further

Another important stage of that maturity is *leadership* in the gifts. Say you are a teacher. You might have started out as assistant teacher on a team, then led a bible study for a small group at your church, then progressed into a lead teacher position. But, eventually, you should become a leader of teachers, teaching others to teach, passing on what you have learned. Scripture is clear that the mature and experienced are to teach and mentor the younger and inexperienced.[58] If we have been serving for years, it is time for us to train the ones who come after us. How else do you think training happens? Who else is going to do it?

We should be maturing. That takes intention. We have to be purposeful to grow.

---

[56] Romans 8:29; 2 Corinthians 3:18
[57] Romans 12:6-8: prophesying, serving, teaching, encourage, giving, lead, show mercy. 1 Corinthians 12:8-10: message of wisdom, message of knowledge, faith, healing, miraculous powers, prophecy, distinguishing between spirits, speaking in different kinds of tongues, and interpretation of tongues
[58] Hebrew 5:12-14; Ephesians 4:11-13

13: BIRDS OF A FEATHER

To get things done, we need to be part of a team. His people as a community founded and operating in love was always God's intention.

No lone rangers, please

We can't do this alone. Not healing, not growing, not serving. Not even living well. We need the support of a community. In particular, we need our sisters in Christ. The importance of a sisterhood cannot be underestimated. We need our sisters to come alongside of us to strengthen and support us. We can't do it by ourselves. The Body of Christ, the community of His people, is God's chosen vehicle through which to work in the world.[59] He has always intended to work through His Body, not through lone individuals. Besides, we get far more done together.

There is something special about the sisterhood we can have in Christ. God has gifted me in that I've always had Christian girlfriends everywhere I've lived. I actively seek them out and work hard to develop those friendships. Those that lasted have been sustained by phone, email, or text as I have moved around. They've been there for me in some of my darkest hours. I am certain that I would not have

---

[59] Ephesians 4:3-5; John 18:22-23

made it through some of the worst times I have had without them.

Because of their love, their support, because they were willing to speak the truth in love, they have also helped me become my best self.

Fake flock

There is a sort of false fellowship that older church women are particularly prone to. They come together, they have refreshments, they do a bit of chatting, but they don't get "real" with each other. It doesn't satisfy the deep soul hunger for authentic connection. How do you know? If you leave feeling unsatisfied, if nothing that happened moved you closer to Christ, if there was no bonding with the other women there, if you left knowing no more about each other than you knew before you came.

Such a gathering is actually like an inoculation against the real thing! It is easy to have such a gathering and think you've done your duty. Paul calls this a "form of godliness without any power."[60]

On the wings of love

But the kind of togetherness I am talking about is a unity of mind and purpose, a real love for each other, a stalwart, I've-got-your-back insistence. Feeling supported, being encouraged, and even being challenged characterizes such a gathering.

In one church I attended, a group of women wanted to seek God for healing of their wounded hearts. This was long before the wealth of resources on inner healing that we have available now. We met weekly, prayed, read Scripture, and shared our lives. We didn't even really know what we needed or what we were doing. But God guided us. The vulnerable, transparent sharing of our lives and the acceptance we gave each other was as valuable as anything else we learned.

---

[60] 2 Timothy 3:5

13: Birds of a Feather

As God's people, our interaction with one another needs to be characterized by Paul's description of love: *Love is patient, love is kind. It does not envy, it does not boast, it is not proud. It does not dishonor others, it is not self-seeking, it is not easily angered, it keeps no record of wrongs. Love does not delight in evil but rejoices with the truth. It always protects, always trusts, always hopes, always perseveres. Love never fails.*[61] This kind of love takes work but it is such a gift when we share it!

A lone duck

I know that loneliness often characterizes the lives of older women. Their husbands have died, their families live far away. A true community centered around God can become (actually *should* be) a family, one that offers unconditional love, support, assistance in time of need — and life-giving fellowship.

So developing a true sisterhood in Christ is also important for the sake of our emotional wellbeing. Loneliness is a desperate and sad condition. True Christian fellowship is the antidote.

Teamwork gets it done

As we age, our physical limitations can increase. But when we work together, we can still get a great deal done in spite of those limits. There is a synergy that comes from working together that brings about results greater than could be achieved by each of us working individually.

Women tend to be better than men about gathering together. They seem to naturally have the skills for community. This is a valuable resource to bring to the Church at large.

One of the coolest stories I have ever heard

I heard about a small group of women in their 80s. Their church had declined so far that the five of them were all that were left. Over

---

[61] 1 Corinthians 13: 4-8

time, the church had dropped all the activities except Sunday morning worship, and now that was in jeopardy because the price for heating oil was rising so high, they couldn't afford to warm the sanctuary for Sunday services.

Participating in a renewal plan offered by their denomination, they learned to think in new ways. They connected with their community, looking for needs that they might be able to meet, and partners with whom they could meet those needs. One need mentioned over and over was the fear that the seniors in the community were especially going to suffer during the coming winter, which was projected to be unusually cold. The high costs of heating oil would particularly affect those on small, fixed incomes. The proposed solution was a warming center — and guess what facility was available! Grants were written to fund the warming center located at the church.

This team of five elderly women turned things around for their own church, as well as for the seniors in the community, and built lasting relationships with other concerned citizens, who were quite impressed with their foresight and wisdom.[62]

It is a miraculous story, but God didn't do this by Himself! Do you know how easy it would have been for those women to decide that there was nothing that could be done, to give up, and let the church close? After all, there were only five of them. And they were old. The community had written the church off a long time ago. Culturally, the women themselves had also been dismissed as unimportant.

But they not only decided to pursue hope, they also engaged in a renewal process that took them decidedly out of their comfort zone. They learned all kinds of new things in the training — and then they went out and *did* what they learned! They took a risk and it paid off

---

[62] Story told by Rev. Glynnis LeBarre, missional strategist for the American Baptist Churches, USA.

handsomely. They stuck together, operated as a team, and, by God's grace, reaped an incredible reward.

There is no reason this story needs to be a one-time event. Versions of this story could be repeated all over our world. *You* could have such a story! Like them, you could become a woman of greatness. God could use you, too, to do something astounding.[63]

Rules of the game for teamwork

Being part of the Community of God means we already have a team. But healthy, effective teamwork is only possible if we lay down our envy, pride, and selfish ambition, give up the need to control, be respectful, welcome diversity, and make room for each woman's gifts and contributions. If we seek Him, God will give us plans and strategies for accomplishing His purposes together. In the Holy Spirit we have a Coach. If we employ teamwork, we can get so much done. Teamwork is vitally important to accomplishing God's Plan.

Because we *are* on the same team, we can't let jealousy and conflict divide us. Women can be catty and divisive, letting silly non-issues interfere. There is no room for barriers based on economic status, racial differences, our husbands' careers, what side of town our house is located on, what denomination we are, how big our church is. We need to be on guard against that. Can you see how silly and superficial all that is in the face of the incredible needs that face us?

Unity centered in the love of Christ is deeply important to God.[64] Christian unity is a sign and wonder to the world around us.[65]

---

[63] If you already have—or develop—a story that should be shared with other FOWLs, please go to the FOWL page on the artofthriving.net website. We want to have a rich resource of the stories to encourage and strengthen and inspire us all.
[64] John 17:23; Ephesians 4:13; Colossians 3:14
[65] John 17:21

Leading the flock

In that vein, I have mentioned that I have been a pastor for several years. Women in churches can be incredibly unsupportive of women in leadership. I've never understood what that is about. It always seemed to me that having women in leadership—those doing a good job—was exciting. Women bring something very different to leadership than men do.

Women in leadership—including as pastor—are more common now. Thankfully, younger generations don't get, let alone promote, the issues the older ones have with women in leadership. It is a complete non-issue for them.

I urge you to be supportive of women in leadership who are doing a good job and following God. It is lonely to be a leader, let alone to be a female leader. To be a female leader in Christian work is *really* hard, so support them.

One heart gathered

It is deeply important that we pray for and work to nurture and develop friendships with Christian women. With women who get the whole following-God thing and have a heart for that. Let's not deny ourselves that support.

If you don't have community, you can start working to form one. Pray that God will bring you flocking together with other women with whom you can be birds of a feather.

14: PERFECT FOWL

One of the terms for Christ's Church is the Bride of Christ.[66] When you read the description in Revelations you can see that She is destined to be spectacular.

It starts with you

Christ's Church is meant to be without spot or stain or wrinkle.[67] Pure, holy, and radiant. Gorgeous.[68] But here's the thing: The *Body* of Christ will not be that beautiful unless and until we, who make up the Bride of Christ, are *ourselves* without spot or stain or wrinkle! We personally are responsible for our walk with God, for our maturity, obedience, holiness, purity, generosity, and love. Individually, we need to be pursuing all those attributes that are to characterize the people of God. They will only be the attributes of the *people* of God if they are *our* attributes as individual daughters of God. Together, all of us walking in righteousness, will be that holy and pure Bride.

---

[66] Revelations 19:7; Revelations 21:9
[67] Ephesians 5:27
[68] Revelation 19:7-8

Role model

It can't be *them* unless it is first *me*. Helping the whole Church get to that place of maturity and beauty comes when we live it out loud, wholeheartedly, right in front of them. We women who belong to God are meant to be a model for the whole Church, a type, a representation of what the Bride of Christ looks like. God wants us individually to be pure and holy, full of His love and light, and then to model that holiness to the world. To demonstrate for the world around us what God can do with a surrendered vessel. If those of us who have been at this a while aren't modeling it to the newbies, who will? It's on us. Not just the world, but the Church needs to see Christ lived out in daily lives.

She's swell

To talk about how we become the radiant Bride, (if you'll forgive me) here is a baseball metaphor. As a player prepares for the big game, he follows steps:

- *Show Up*. Put yourself before God. Come into His presence. Draw near. Spend time with Him.
- *Shower up*. Get cleaned up. Wash in the Blood of the Lamb[69] and be forgiven for your sins. Deal with the garbage in your souls, with the rubble in your life.
- *Suit up*. Put on the nature, mind,[70] and character of Christ.[71] Put on the armor of the Holy Spirit.[72]
- *Step up*. Head toward God. Don't hold back. Say yes to God. Practice obedience.
- *Swing*. Do the work you are called, trained, and positioned to do.

---

[69] Revelations 7:14
[70] 1 Corinthians 2:16
[71] Ephesians 4:24; Romans 13:14
[72] Ephesian 6:11-16

I urge you to be a worthy representative of the Bride of Christ. Do your part to be the Bride yourself. Let Christ be spectacularly displayed in you.

Fat Old White Lady

15: UNDER THE SHELTER OF HIS WING

There is a reason that sisterhood in Christ is so powerful. There is a reason that the Bride of Christ is called to be spectacular. The reason is relationship.

Family ties

Did you know that, even before Creation was created, God desired relationship? God is perfect in Himself. He exists in perfect relationship with Himself—Father, Son, and Holy Spirit. He has no needs. He is utterly complete, whole, and perfect. But—He *wanted* relationship with someone who was capable of relationship with Him.

That was His purpose in creating Creation. He is a creative God, He delights in creating, so He found pleasure in the creating for its own sake. But His purpose, His goal, was to create independent, self-aware beings, able to think and choose freely—who could chose to be in relationship with Him. [73]

Before and after

In the Garden of Eden, before the Fall, this relationship existed, free and unfettered.[74] But the sin and disobedience of Adam and Eve

---
[73] Genesis 1:26
[74] Genesis 3:8 God and Adam and Eve were accustomed to walking together in fellowship.

ended that idyll. And humanity has been far from God ever since.[75]

So God did what was necessary to restore His beloved children to relationship with Him. Sending His Son to die on the cross for our sins was radical. It was done from a depth of love that is inconceivable. But it *was* done in love, and it was done in order to restore us to relationship with Him.[76]

An author described what He was aiming for: *He knew that the cost for raising sons and daughters mature enough to give Him adult fellowship, person-to-Person, would have to be His own suffering through the death of His only begotten Son on the cross.*[77]

This is truly an astounding concept. It blows me away! God wants friends! If we will heal, leave sin behind, grow to maturity, we can become friends of God.

Building blocks

Like any relationship, it takes time together, effort, listening, sharing, commitment, giving way to the needs and desires of the other. If you had a great marriage, you have a glimpse of what this relationship with God is to be—and how to work on it and develop it. Scripture is clear that marriage between a husband and wife is a type, an earthly representation of this heavenly marriage of the Bride and Her Groom.[78] What we have learned in and from earthly marriage can help us understand how to be in and develop our relationship with God.

Of course, He made the first move. He reached out to us in his Son, He gave to us so generously in the gift of salvation through

---

[75] Isaiah 59:2; Ephesians 2:12
[76] I John 3:1
[77] Jackson, John Paul. Needles Casualties of War. Streams Publications: Sutton, New Hampshire, 1999. Forward by John Sanford.
[78] Ephesians 5:21-33; Revelation 21:9-11

15: Under the Shelter of His Wings

Christ's death on the Cross, giving us righteousness and right standing with Him. The Holy Spirit comes to be God in us.

But, like a young woman accepting a marriage proposal, we have to say yes. We have to respond to this love with love of our own. We have to commit ourselves to this relationship.

Part of our recovery from the effects of sin and damage, part of serving in obedience, and essential to fulfilling and completing us, is establishing ourselves in this relationship of love.

This love, this relationship, is the foundation of everything else in this book, of the *Missio Dei*, of the work of serving the world, working to make a difference.

Fat Old White Lady

WHAT TRULY MATTERS

We are called into the eternally significant work that God is doing and invites us into. His Kingdom is advancing and we get to be a part of that work! There is quite literally nothing more important, significant, or eternal than that. There is too much work to do to have someone taken off the team simply for gender, age, race, weight, or other irrelevancies. The perception that FOWLs have nothing to contribute is completely false. For God's work, it does not matter how old, attractive, slim, or rich we are.

It. Does. Not. Matter!

What matters is our heart. Our obedience. Our love. We already have in us all that is worthwhile and valuable — because we have God there! We need to ignore the cultural mandates defining worth, and get the job done. We are not helpless. We are not useless. In fact, we can be formidable. We are capable of far more than we think.

Fat Old White Lady

SECTION THREE WORKBOOK

Core Principle: Treasures of Darkness
1. Examine how you have responded to the negative, hurtful things that have happened to you in your life. Was your response positive and productive, a response that allowed you to move forward? Or was it negative and debilitating, keeping you wounded and damaged? Do you see a pattern in your responses to more than one difficult event? Would you like to take steps to turn your negative response around to something that allows you to move forward in a positive way?
2. Can you find yourself in the Joseph story? What part particularly speaks to you? Can you see God refining, training, or positioning you? Are you willing to let Him start to do that now?

FOWL Fritters
3. Look at how you spend your time. Are you wasting a lot of time in meaningless pursuits? If so, why is that? Does the challenge to make your life count for something connect with you? What changes could you make so that more of your time is spent on something meaningful?
4. Do you have the attitude: Eat, drink, and be merry, for tomorrow we die? If so, why? How does the realization that we have eternity with God following this life change things for you?
5. Do you think it is true that *purpose* comes from having a goal, a direction, and *meaning* is found in making a contribution, making a difference, and that we can find *fulfillment* in expressing our passions and using our gifts? If that is true, what changes could you make so that you could find more meaning, purpose, and fulfillment in your life?

FOWL Air

6. Have you made a concerted effort to be a person who is always growing? Or have you gotten stagnant, dull, uninspired? Could you take a step this week to learn something fresh and different?

7. Have you gotten outside of your routine and rut lately? Have you read a significant book in the past year? Have you tried a new ethnic restaurant? Gone to a presentation to learn something new? Have you tried a new form of prayer? Gone to a spiritual retreat? Consider trying one of these ideas or something else that is new to you that gets you out of your routine; something that offers a fresh new perspective. Recruit a partner who can brave new paths with you.

8. Has Christ been formed in you? Or do you currently exhibit any of the following?

Gossiper	Fearful
Negative	Judgmental
Resentful	Easily offended
Controlling	Prideful
Critical spirit	Angry
Victim mentality	

Is it time to deal with the state of your heart?

- ❏ Come before God in earnest sorrow for the mess in your heart
- ❏ Agree with Him that you need to change and ask Him for the help to do so
- ❏ Study the following scriptures for guidance on the kind of behavior you ought to demonstrate: Galatians 5:22; John 3:30; Romans 5:3-5; Philippians 2:1-11; Matthew 5:1-10

Utilize some tools to help you with your change:

- ❏ Create some affirmations that declare the new you
- ❏ Every time you have a thought that you don't want, toss it into God's Buglight in the Sky

- ❏ Ask an accountability partner to point out when you revert to this unwanted behavior
- ❏ Keep a journal, reflecting on the changes you know you need to make, and on the things that happen, seeking to learn from them.

9. Is there a subject you have always wanted to learn more about or something you've always wanted to do but haven't yet? Why not take a step in that direction, starting this week? There are many sources of learning including books at the public library, a course at the community college or adult education program, an online course. Could you find training so you could learn it?

10. Have you figured out what your spiritual gifts are yet? If not, take steps to take one or more spiritual gifts assessments this week. It is fun to gain that kind of self-knowledge, but it also gives you useful information. It shows you how you might serve. Then you can start looking for where. If you do a search online, you can find many free spiritual gifts assessments. Below are some that I found. (Please note that I make no claims about or recommendations for these tests.) These won't all agree in every aspect. Take more than one and look for the commonalities.

    http://www.spiritualgiftstest.com/
    https://gifts.churchgrowth.org/cgi-cg/gifts.cgi?intro=1
    http://mintools.com/spiritual-gifts-test.htm

11. Are you actively working to become a mature Christian? If not, why not? Could you take a step in that direction by attending a Bible study or setting aside time each day to pray? For centuries, Christians have practiced spiritual disciplines as a way of developing spiritually.

Consider trying one of the following practices as a way of opening up your spiritual life to God in a fresh way:

- ❏ *Intercession*: Pray for the needs of others.
- ❏ *Lectio divina*. Read a scripture passage, sit with it, reflect on it, and ask God to speak to you through it.
- ❏ *Fasting*. Abstain from something (this could be all food, a certain category or type of food, entertainment, a bad habit), accompanied by prayer for a period of time for the purpose of drawing closer to God.
- ❏ *Giving alms*. Give money to help the poor.
- ❏ *Tithing*. Give a regular amount to the care and support of your local church.
- ❏ *Service*. Help the neediest and poorest in Christ's name. Help with needs in your church and community.
- ❏ *Study scriptures*. Use or attend a bible study.
- ❏ *Meditation*. Think deeply and spiritually about a scriptural truth, an attribute of God's character, Creation.
- ❏ *Simplicity*. Practice intentional non-consumption.
- ❏ *Worship*.
- ❏ *Repentance*.
- ❏ *Forgiveness*.

12. Have you ever considered that part of your responsibility as a mature Christian is to pass on what you know to those who come after you? Have you or are you currently doing any mentoring or training? Might you be willing to step up to do so now?

Birds of a Feather

13. Do you have fellowship with other women? If not, why not? How would you describe the fellowship you do have? Is it real or is it fairly superficial? What steps could you take to develop or improve your sisterhood to the degree that it satisfies your heart and enables you to accomplish God's purposes together? Can you find other like-minded women who share that desire and work together with them?

Section Three Workbook

14. Does loneliness characterize your life? Do you agree that Christian community, a sisterhood of fellow believers in Christ, could become a family, a source of belonging? Are you willing to make the effort to find that community?

15. Have you ever experienced the synergy of a true team? Could you work to form a team to address a problem in your community?

Perfect FOWL

16. Are you pursuing holiness and purity? Why or why not? What does that look like in your life? What has helped you to do that?

17. If you, as a woman — and especially as an older, more mature Christian woman — were to truly be a role model for the Church on how to be the Bride of Christ, what changes would you need to make in your life, your actions, your word in order to be a godly and effective role model? Is that something you are willing to do?

18. Examine the church you attend. Does it show to the community around you how spectacular Christ's Bride is? If not, what could be done to change that?

Under the Shelter of His Wing

19. Have you ever considered the notion that God created humanity because He wanted friends? How does that make you feel? Does it change anything? What changes would you need to make if you wanted to be a mature, adult friend of God?

20. Have you already or are you willing to put in the time, attention, and effort it takes to have a friendship with God?

21. What could your marriage teach you about being in relationship with God?

22. Go through the footnoted scriptures. Look at them in the context used in this book. What did you learn? Did you change an opinion? Will you now change an action?

Fat Old White Lady

SECTION FOUR: SERVICE

If you think you are finished, I hope you will think again! God is not finished with you yet. Hopefully, by the end of this section, that revelation will be astonishingly good news.

Fat Old White Lady

CORE PRINCIPLE: ON GOD'S TEAM

There are two parts to the mission of God — to the *Missio Dei* — both of which are important. God wants to make our *individual* life whole and healed. To set all things right in our lives personally. And He also wants to set things right throughout the *whole world*. As God's beloved children, called into His Mission, we get to be a part of that.

We can line up with the will of God when we participate in His Main Thing. We don't have to be sidelined. We have a place to be, a job to do. We get to join in the most exciting, the most significant work there ever was or ever will be. The main thing going on is God, and His main work is the *Missio Dei*.[79]

And we get to be a part of it. We get to be on God's Team. We get to be crewmates with God. He calls us to co-labor with Him in His Plan to set all things right.[80]

So, how do we participate?

What, where, and how?

What we each have to offer. We have been created with talents, have developed skills, with a lifetime of experiences. God gave them

---

[79] Daniel 4:3; 2 Peter 1:11
[80] 1 Corinthians 3:9; 2 Corinthians 6:1

to us to use.[81] Our spiritual gifts are also meant to be used. Not only do we have the gifts God put inside of each of us, but we also have our passions—those things that get our juices flowing. And we have a vast reservoir of experience. All that we've done and all that we know can come to bear on what we do now. Truly, never before in the history of the world have so many middle-aged and older women had so many resources available to them! Many of us likely have a home, education and training, time, and finances. We also have relationships and spiritual maturity. We can put all of this into His service.

Where we offer it. There are some areas of profound influence in our culture: Media, Arts and Entertainment, Education, Government, Family, Religion and Spirituality, and Commerce/Business. These are institutions of existence, spheres of influence that are far bigger than any one individual. They have a life of their own, spanning multiple generations.

If we seek to serve God, our call will take place in one of these areas. That is where we can go and do God's work.

How we offer it. Be salt and light.[82] Salt is a preservative that keeps food from spoiling, a seasoning that brings out flavors in food, a healing agent, and it creates thirst. We can bring those salty attributes into whatever we do, and we can do work that accomplishes these actions: preserving, seasoning, healing, creating thirst (for God and Hs goodness). Salt is absorbed into food and the body, and works from the inside.

Light shines onto something. It illuminates, warms, reveals, clarifies. Our good words and good deeds are forms of light. We can shine the light of Christ into our work, our relationships, our neighborhood—anywhere in our daily world.

---

[81] Matthew 25:14-30
[82] Matthew 5:13-16

Core Principle: On God's Team

We are called to be salt and light in one of the spheres of influence. That is how we co-labor with God.

What do we do? There is a list that gives us a good place to start. *For I was hungry and you gave me something to eat, I was thirsty and you gave me something to drink, I was a stranger and you invited me in, I needed clothes and you clothed me, I was sick and you looked after me, I was in prison and you came to visit me.*[83] Jesus is very clear that addressing these needs is part of following Him.

If we seek Him, He will lead us. Our passions, our gifts, and the opportunities right in front of us will also help to guide us.

Even if

You may feel that there is so much wrong with you that you will never be able to offer anything. But God heals. He restores, redeems, rescues. He doesn't throw away. One of my favorite movie lines comes from *Seabiscuit*.[84] Tom Smith says, "You know, you don't throw a whole life away just 'cause he's banged up a little." God doesn't either. We need to work on our healing and serve where we can. As we heal further, new opportunities for service will come.

Donbee; doobee

You don't have to earn your way into God's good graces by being good. (We cover that in *The Roost*, later in Section Four.) But God is Good,[85] He does Good,[86] and He invites you to do Good, too.[87] When you do God's Good work, you are His partner in His Creation-wide work of restoration, recovery, and transformation.

Don't be a Good Girl, but do Good, girl!

---

[83] Matthew 25:31-46; Romans 12:6-8
[84] *Seabiscuit*, Universal Pictures, Dreamworks, Spyglass Entertainment, 2003.
[85] Mark 10:18
[86] Psalm 100:5; Psalm 106:1
[87] Deuteronomy 6:18; Ps 34:14; 37.3; Romans 2:7,10; 2 Thessalonians 3:13; Titus 3:8; Ephesians 2:10

Fat Old White Lady

16: WELL-FED FOWL

Are you over-fed and under-worked? You are if you are not actively applying what you have learned from God.

Hear AND do

Over the years in different churches, I have seen women who have been in Bible study in church for years and years. They love God's Word. Of course, there is nothing wrong with that! Although this type of woman is a dying breed (because fewer and fewer younger women have any interest in Bible study, let alone the time to pursue it in a group), there are many women who have been engaged in Bible study in groups and on their own, as well as listening to sermons every week—for years. They have a rich understanding and depth of knowledge.

The problem is often that I don't see much evidence of them *applying* what they have learned into their daily lives! Not in the choices they make, the way they relate to each other, handle difficulties, or reach out in ministry to the community around them.

If we are a *hearer* of God's word but not a *doer* of God's word, we are missing the point.[88] Hearing but not doing is just a form of ignoring. Ignoring God is not a great idea![89]

Know it = do it

See, the thing is, if we *know* it, God holds us accountable for *applying* it![90] Knowing and not doing is actually *worse* than not knowing.[91] Not knowing is ignorance, whereas knowing and not doing is disobedience.[92] Yikes!

If we have been soaking up God's word in Bible studies and sermons for years, what are we doing with that knowledge? Are we putting any of it into practice? In the cautionary parable about the sheep and the goats in Matthew 25, Jesus says, "Whatever you did for the least of these you did for Me." Have we taken care of the poor, and the sick, and the needy, and the ones in prison? A strikingly similar chapter in Isaiah 58 powerfully states that if we don't do what God commands, if we are not concerned about the things God is concerned about, we are out of His will.

Teaching ought to lead to *training* which ought to lead to *doing*. Most of us now need doing far more than we need more teaching.

Don't be well-fed and underworked. Where does God want you to serve Him? Where can you apply the riches you have stored up in your heart?

---

[88] Luke 6:48-49 (Mess); James 1:22-25
[89] Matthew 21:28031
[90] Romans 2:13; James 4:17
[91] Matthew 7:21
[92] Luke 12:47-48; James 2:14-26

17: FEATHERING YOUR NEST

It is not acceptable for everything in our life to be about us—our own comfort, our own happiness and wellbeing.

Blessed to be a blessing

From the time God first called Abraham up to today, God's people have been blessed so that they can be a blessing.[93] You and I are blessed in order to be a blessing to others. God calls us to give, to be generous, to help those in need.[94] There is very little in Scripture about how God wants us to be happy and satisfied.[95] (Those come at times as we walk with God, but they are not the goal.) In fact, being too smug and self-satisfied is a warning sign that something is badly out of whack![96] Jesus was pretty clear that storing up treasure for ourselves when there is need around us is wrong—and foolish.[97]

Mothers know the art of blessing others. They sacrifice themselves all the time, all day long, for the sake of their children's wellbeing. That skill needs to be extended to all of God's children, to all

---

[93] Genesis 22:17-18
[94] 2 Corinthians 9:8
[95] Romans 15:1-5
[96] Luke 12:15-21
[97] Luke 12:33-34

those in need.

If we are going to think of ourselves as blessed to be a blessing, we are going to be counter-culture. Everything around us screams loudly the importance of getting more and more stuff, of being selfish and self-absorbed. Our North American culture encourages the pursuit of possessions, bling, comfort, and impressing others. But that is not what God says is important. His measure of value has nothing to do with stuff. As people belonging to God, it is important that we bring our use of money, our time, and ourselves before God and ask Him how He wants us to spend it. We are blessed by whatever we have. All good things come from God.[98]

It's not all about you

Now, God loves each of us. That is deeply, profoundly true. He wants to heal us, be deeply present in our lives, help us to thrive. So that part is about us. But God's mission in the world is not to make us comfortable. Or even happy. (Joy, however, is promised in abundance.[99]) God's mission is about changing everything: fixing what is broken, freeing the captives, making the blind see, and the lame walk.[100] God is about a Big Picture view of setting all things right — the *Missio Dei*.

The only pursuit in the world that is truly worth giving our entire life and self to is seeking God and His Kingdom. All else wears out, fades, falls away. Jesus reminded us to store up our treasures in heaven, not somewhere here on earth.[101] That is why it is not acceptable to spend everything we have, all of our blessings — on ourselves. God blesses us to be a blessing

---

[98] James 1:17
[99] Psalm 16:11; Psalm 51:12; Isaiah 12:3; Isaiah 55:12; John 15:11
[100] Isaiah 61:1-3
[101] Matthew 6:19-21

18: THE ROOST

You aren't meant to carry the load by yourself. God has provided a safe haven, a place of peace, an opportunity to rest—a roost.

Called to rest

There is work we are called to do. And we need to give it everything we've got. But we are not meant to be burdened by work that is *not* ours to do. In fact, Jesus was quite clear about that. *Come to me, all you who are weary and burdened, and I will give you rest. Take my yoke upon you and learn from me, for I am gentle and humble in heart, and you will find rest for your souls. For my yoke is easy and my burden is light.*[102] And God is clear that we are not on our own; He helps us to do His will.[103]

Much of the time, the incredible burden we feel is because we are trying to be in control. That is a battle we can't win! There is too much outside of our control—like other people, circumstance, and outcomes, to name a few. The good news is that God *is* in control. He can do what we cannot. He invites us to relinquish things beyond our control to Him and to rest in His care.

---

[102] Matthew 11:28-29
[103] Philippians 2:13

We need to stop fretting and fussing over the things that we can't control. We are responsible for our choices, thoughts, attitudes, actions, and for doing the work we are given to do. But we need to take a chill pill and relinquish it all to God. Let Him give us our assignments, let Him give us strength and grace to do them, let Him guide our steps. Learn to roost our hearts in His Shalom.

The bad news and the good news

There is another area where we are invited to rest in God's roost that the world doesn't know, and many Christians seem either to have never known or have forgotten. Have you heard the question: *If you were to die today and were to stand before the Apostle Peter at the Pearly Gates, and he asked you, "Why should I let you into God's Heaven?"*[104] *what would you say?*

What would *you* say? Some typical answers I have heard include:

- I have tried to be a good person.
- I have done more good things than bad.
- I rescued my friend when he was drowning. That ought to count for something.
- I have attended church for most of my life.

Would it surprise you to find out that *none* of those answers would satisfy ol' Pete and get you past those beautiful gates into Heaven? **None. Of. Them.** That is because each of those answers imply that we can be good enough, do something good enough, to be accepted into Heaven on our own merits—and the bad news is, we simply can't be good enough to *earn* our way into God's good graces.

The Jews had the Law. It described everything they had to do to be in right standing before God. It was very clear and explicit. There was no other way to be right before God. And in spite of millennia of trying, those folks—the Chosen People of God—had never been able

---

[104] Diagnostic question from Evangelism Explosion training (evangelismexplosion.org)

18: The Roost

to keep the whole Law. Most of the time, they didn't come close. And there were many times when they wandered far, far away and weren't even remotely on the same page as God.

The good news is that God took care of that for us. That is the whole point of Jesus coming, living, and dying.[105] God knew that we were broken by sin and hounded and terrified by death.[106] So He devised a plan to fix things so that He could get us right with Him—a plan that didn't require any effort of our own. He had planned and worked toward this for some time. (That is the *Missio Dei*.) Finally, when the time was right, He sent His very precious and beloved Son, Jesus. Jesus did everything right according to the Law, fulfilled every requirement (something no Jew had ever been able to achieve). Then He died—shedding His own blood as an offering, fulfilling all the requirements of the Law—in our place, for our sake,[107] receiving the punishment we deserved for screwing up so badly, for going so far away from God's will. God did the entire thing himself, wrapped it up in a bow, and gave it to us as a gift. All we have to do is accept it.[108]

That is why we don't have to do anything to earn that right standing. We can't. Instead, God took care of it; He did it for us. That is why, in answer to that question about why God should let us into Heaven, detailing all the good things we did won't cut it. That isn't the answer.

The only answer is: *Lord God, I accept what You did through Your Son's death on the cross. I accept the right standing You made possible. You let me into Your Heaven because You love me and Your Son loves me. And, boy, am I so very, very grateful!* That's it.

---

[105] Acts 5:30-31
[106] Hebrews 2:15
[107] Romans 4:26; Ephesians 2:1-5; 1 Peter 2:24
[108] Ephesians 2:8-9

The right kind of good

It is Good Girl thinking to feel that we have to be doing something all the time. It is easy to transfer that sense of obligation and duty onto God. So many of us feel that we have to be good, do more and more good, in order to make God pleased with us. This is a horrible, terrible, very bad burden and we need to offload it *right now!* We must stop being a Good Girl.

Not only can we stop being a Good Girl, trying to placate God with our efforts. This gift of right standing that God gives us also sets us free from anything that our society tries to put on us. We are acceptable because God has accepted us! And that has nothing to do with our weight, age, race, or gender. God's gift bypasses all of that, making it utterly irrelevant.

The Roost is all about resting from all that pressure. We do not have to be good enough to earn God's love. Jesus was Good on our behalf. God gives us that Goodness, free of charge, to wear as our very own.

But then His Holy Spirit works that Goodness *into* our hearts and lives, changing us from the inside out.

This means that we can be at peace, a bird come home to the safe nest. Give up the Good Girl nonsense and receive the beautiful present our wonderful Father offers us.

19: WATER FOWL

As a Christ-follower, you are a creature of the water — the water of the Holy Spirit. The water of the Word.[109] You are "water FOWL."

We need Him

Jesus said that streams of living water would flow out of our belly.[110] He meant that the Holy Spirit would be given to us. This is because we *need* the Holy Spirit. God does His work in our lives, in our hearts, through His Holy Spirit. God does His work in the world through us by the power of the Holy Spirit. I talked in *Core Principle: Healing the Wounded Heart* how the work of the Holy Spirit is essential for the full healing of our hearts. The Holy Spirit is also the source of supernatural power and strength for doing the work of God in the world.

One of my favorite verses is: *It is not by might, not by power, but by My Spirit, says the Lord of hosts.*[111] This is so reassuring because it is not up to us to do God's work or the right thing on our own, in our own strength. If we try, at our very best, our efforts will be very small.

---
[109] Ephesians 5:26
[110] John 7:38-39
[111] Zechariah 4:6

Most of the time we won't get anywhere. But God's power in us will accomplish astounding things.

God wants to partner with us. He wants to co-labor.[112] He does that by His Holy Spirit in us, doing in us and through us what we can't do ourselves. We still participate, but it is not totally up to us.

We can't do what needs to be done in the world by ourselves, in our own wisdom, our own power, our own understanding. We need to be women full of the Spirit.

A wee bit leery?

Different Christian groups have had what I personally consider odd relationships with the Holy Spirit. Certain branches of Christians claim that anything to do with the Holy Spirit belongs solely in the ancient past. Then there are others who know (or suspect) that there is a Holy Spirit, but have no idea what to make of Him. Some are scared stiff of what they've seen or imagined. Others are embarrassed by something so frankly supernatural and unscientific. For many of these folks, avoidance or denial has seemed the best policy.

I bring this subject up because *you need the Holy Spirit*. And if that feels threatening or intimidating, it might be because you have been part of one of those streams of thought that has an awkward relationship with the Holy Spirit. I invite you to let go of expectations or anything that has characterized your experience previously. You can safely be open to what the Holy Spirit wants to do in your life and through you in the world.

What He does

The Third Person of the Trinity (Father, Son, and Holy Spirit) offers God's power, guidance, grace, and strength. Jesus promised that the Holy Spirit would be our counselor, our teacher, our comforter.[113]

---

[112] 1 Corinthians 3:9
[113] John 14:6

He tells us what God is doing.[114] The Spirit teaches us the truth, and gives us spiritual gifts[115] that enable us to do, in a supernatural way, what we could not do in our own strength. We *need* that if we are going to do God's work in the world. We can't do it by ourselves. It's too big; it's beyond us. We need the Holy Spirit.

The Holy Spirit makes one Body out of disparate people. The Holy Spirit is like lubricating oil; He smooths the way between people. He can bring us into a unity that is simply supernatural.[116] (Seeing the way our world seems to be more and more divided over every kind of line imaginable, you know that unity *must* be a supernatural act!) He can guide us together into His work in the world. He is our lamp, the illumination in our minds and hearts. He is the One who brings people into relationship with God and the salvation He offers.[117] (No one is saved without the Holy Spirit.) He directs our worship of and toward God.[118]

The Spirit at work in us is God at work in the world.

We must all be water FOWL. The Mission of God requires us to be women of the Spirit. So let God pour rivers of living water through you, out of your innermost parts, into the world.

---

[114] 1 Corinthians 2:10-16
[115] Romans 12:4-8; 1 Corinthians 1:7-11; Ephesian 4:11-12
[116] Ephesians 4:3, 13; 1 Corinthians 12:12-14; 1 Corinthians 10:17
[117] Ephesians 1:13; 6:10-17 Titus 3:5
[118] 1 Corinthians 12:3

Fat Old White Lady

20: LAYING THE GOLDEN EGG

Do you remember the slogan in the 80s? PBPGINFWMY: Please Be Patient, God Is Not Finished With Me Yet. It was a way of affirming that, while we are not perfect, God is still at work in us. But *God Is Not Finished with Me Yet* also applies to what God wants to do *through* you. You know that God is not finished working through you yet, right? He doesn't think that you are done being useful, finished making a difference.

It ain't over 'til it's over

That's the truth. We may be past childbearing age; our kids may have left home. We may be retired from our job. We may be elderly. We may even be disabled. But God is not finished with us yet.

Not only is He not finished working *in* us, conforming us into the likeness of His Son, but He is not finished with us doing His work *in the world*. (Of course, this all depends on whether we allow Him to do that work! We can refuse to allow God access to us and He will allow that.) Basically, we are not done until God says we're done.

I know that parts of us dry up with menopause. But *we* didn't dry up along with our dry parts! If we have kept our hearts tender toward

God, we are good soil for God's seed,[119] and God can still do His work in us and through us. (And if our heart has gotten hard, we can ask Him to soften it.[120])

Remaining riches

Do you remember the fable of the goose that laid the golden egg?

One day a countryman going to the nest of his goose found there an egg all yellow and glittering. When he took it up it was as heavy as lead and he was going to throw it away, because he thought a trick had been played upon him. But on second thought he took it home, and soon found to his delight that it was an egg of pure gold. Every morning the same thing occurred, and he soon became rich by selling his eggs. But as he grew rich he grew greedy; and thinking to get at once all the gold the goose could give, he killed it and opened it only to find — nothing.

If we don't let circumstances break our hearts, or get trapped by society's expectations for our time in life, or let the opinions of others take us out, we still have much to give. Life didn't end when our kids left the home or we retired. We are still capable of bringing forth gold, and God wants us to give it to the world.

I know a woman who retired from a government job (during which she lived in many places around the world). She is now deeply involved in her church, serving in various positions of leadership. But perhaps even more importantly, she serves in various places in the community — volunteering in the office that offers assistance to people in need, on an ideas committee for dealing with local issues between Native Americans and the larger white community, and a couple of other civic boards. Retirement for her has meant more opportunities

---

[119] Matthew 13:3-23
[120] Ezekiel 11:19

to serve. She is putting her breadth of experience and skills to good use.

Making excuses

On the other hand, it is very easy to dismiss ourselves from participating in God's work. I know a leader who is calling for people to become part of something God is doing. She met weekly with groups in different towns, praying for revival. Part of the preparation was training in discipleship. This leader is full of the Holy Spirit and operates powerfully in the prophetic, and she knows that God is preparing people for what is to come.

Although the folks declared that they felt called by God to be there, over time, several stopped coming. One woman said, "I have a new puppy and it is on a schedule, so I can't get away." Another woman had a tire blow out and became afraid to drive, so she didn't come anymore. Another woman didn't want to come by herself. For various reasons, they each dismissed themselves.

On this side of things, what is going to happen is a complete unknown. But on the other side, when God has done something truly amazing, can you imagine how they will feel to have missed out on being a part of it? Jesus told a similar parable.[121] He wasn't very impressed with excuses!

The old girl's still got it

If you would still like to make a difference, make a contribution, be part of the solution, I hope that knowing that God isn't finished with you yet makes you as excited as it does me. You *can* still make a difference! God *wants* you to! There is a world of hurt out there and He wants to minister to every single part of it. That's where we come in — working as His hands and feet, each of us reaching out and doing Good in our little corner of the world.

---

[121] Luke 14:15-24

Some modest suggestions for laying gold

Intercession. There are not enough intercessors praying for the issues and needs in our world today. A lot of people won't take the time or don't have the patience.

There was a picture of the power of intercessors in a book I once read.[122] There is the advancing army of God in an arrowhead formation. At the point of the wedge are the leaders. They are out front, directly confronting the enemy, warriors in the thick of battle. But behind that wedge are the intercessors, lobbing bombs out in front, clearing the ground of the enemy before the advance team even gets there. That is one of the ways intercessors serve. Preparing the way for ministry. Praying for the ministry of others — to clear the way, remove the enemy, and give strength to those leaders. And most of all, praying for the will of God to be done.

There are not enough intercessors doing intercession for the ministries that are trying to carry out God's work! Nor praying for revival fires to burn once again across our land. This is no small or insignificant thing. It is not a case of, "I can't do anything else so I guess I'll pray." There may be a genuine call on your life to pray for the ministries God assigns you to. If so, you are a warrior engaging in the most significant of battles. This prayer can be done even if you are disabled. You can always pray.[123]

Throughout the Bible there are many instances of people interceding in prayer at significant moments in time. Abraham begged God to spare Sodom.[124] King Hezekiah, about to die, asked God for 15 more years.[125] Jesus prayed before selecting His 12 apostles.[126]

---

[122] Joyner, Rick. *The Vision*. NC: MorningStar Publication, 2000.
[123] The movie *War Room* vividly demonstrates the power of intercession. If you haven't seen it, please do! (Kendrick Brothers Productions, 2015.)
[124] Genesis 19
[125] 2 Kings 20:1-11
[126] Luke 6:13

20: Laying the Golden Egg

Prayer is encouraged throughout the New Testament.[127] In more recent times, stories are told about the fabled intercessors for some of the centuries' greatest revivalists.[128]

In addition to praying for ministry leaders like the pastors of our churches or heads of ministries, there is a desperate need for prayer for the civic institutions that affect the lives of so many people. For example, we could build relationships with the mayor, the police chief, or the county commissioner, and offer to pray regularly and specifically for the concerns they raise. We could organize into neighborhood groups to pray for those who live around us.

The one single issue that will have a profound effect on the future of our country and world is our youth. We need to pray for the schools, for those youth addicted to drugs, for those in foster care, for adoptive homes to take in the orphans and give them a forever home (and for those homes that do take in children), for those homes with broken parents that turn out broken children.

If we take this on, we need take our assignment seriously. Make a plan, keep track, check in and get fresh information on the subjects of our prayers.

Grandmother. There are always grandmothers needed in this world. There are so many grandmothers who are raising their grandkids because the kids' parents got into drugs or prison. You probably either are one or know one. Those women are unsung heroes. But there are far too many kids who *don't* have a grandparent present and able to love them.

I have a friend who is in her late 70's. She has befriended a 15-year-old boy who comes to church on his own. Most Sundays she takes him to lunch after church. As she works to build a relationship,

---

[127] Romans 12:12; Ephesians 6:18; Philippians 4:16; James 5:13-18
[128] For a great description of the intercessory ministry of Daniel Nash, who prayed for revivalist Charles Finney, see http://hopefaithprayer.com/prayernew/prevailing-prince-prayer-daniel-nash/

he is starting to trust her with information about his pretty messed up life. She listens with interest and loves on him. Then she goes home and prays for him. Can you imagine the impact her time and interest is having on him at this vulnerable time in his life! (Sadly, the other women her age in church criticize her because she isn't having lunch with *them*. Nor will they join her because, "Those boys are too noisy." Thankfully, she just keeps doing what she is doing, anyway.)

I know a man who had such a woman in his life as a young boy. He was born blind into a poor family in a culture where blindness was a reason to disparage and reject. One day, for no conscious reason, he wandered into church. This older woman (she was 72 at the time) talked to him. He came back. She invited him into her home and fed him. (Since food was in short supply at home, he was always hungry.) And she talked to him about Jesus. When he eventually became a Christ follower, she was the only person present at his baptism. In his early years as a believer, she was his spiritual mother, grounding him in Christ. That man went on to get two Master's degrees and a doctorate in seminary, write five books, be an associate pastor, and start a real estate business! He is now a motivational speaker sharing how Scripture has answers for thriving in life. This woman helped set him on the right path early in his life. Her involvement and kindness made all the difference.

This world needs "adoptive" grandmothers who are willing to step into kids' lives. There are so many absent, wounded, or dysfunctional parents. So many kids without any solid mature Christian person speaking into their lives. We could do that. If there is a family in our church or neighborhood who are raising fostered or adopted kids, we could offer to come alongside to be a part of the child's nurturing system. Just love them and be present and interested. Volunteer at a nearby school to meet with a troubled kid for an hour or two every week. Just spend time with them and love on them. (It isn't rocket science.)

Mentor. For a variety of reasons, there are so many young women who don't know how to be mothers, wives, or even women. They have no clue. Befriending them and offering guidance and support, formally through a program or informally as a neighbor, could make an incredible difference to their marriage and children.[129]

I truly think that if senior women would do even just these three things—we could change the world! The impact of this kind of work would be lasting and potent.

Some additional suggestions less modest and more bold

Maybe the ideas I mentioned above sound too typical for senior women. They don't get you excited. I know that among the women reading this book, there is an incredible, startling, and tremendously powerful pool of talents, skills, and resources. So let's be bold and think outside of the box a bit:

Artist. Write worship songs that your church can sing. Or paint during worship under the inspiration of the Holy Spirit in response to the sermon or time of worship. Write a story that teaches young people the truth about the battle of good and evil and challenges them to live for the Light.

Evangelist. Intentionally build relationships so that you can share the love of God with someone. If you have the prophetic gift, do prophetic evangelism on your city's streets.

Helps. If you have accounting skills, offer help to low-income and/or second-language people with their taxes. If you can plan and organize, offer your help to plan an outreach event. You may not be able to do all the legwork yourself anymore, but the ability to plan and organize is still essential to getting anything done.

Prayer minister. Get trained to offer healing prayer at church and

---

[129] Titus 2:3-4

other gatherings.[130] Offer to pray for people in a booth at a local civic event so that they can hear from God.

Just get started

If you are uncertain what to do, it doesn't hurt to just try some things out. Don't commit yourself to anything long-term right away. Try what sound interesting and see what develops.

Use your creativity. *We cannot solve our problems with the same thinking we used when we created them.*[131] Creativity is at the heart of God, and we are made in His image. (Remember, He is **Creator**. This incredibly beautiful and amazing universe we live in was His idea.) Do some "cross-pollination," that is, use something that worked in one area and try applying it to another area to solve a problem there. You have a vast reservoir of experience. Put it to work in new and innovative ways.

But maybe there has been a whisper deep in your heart, something that has called to you—maybe for a long time. If so, pull that whisper out into the open and look at it. It may be the dream that God has given you, and now may be the time to act on it.

In any case, ask God what He wants you to do. He is glad to guide you. Make it your goal to be like the Boy Scouts: Leave your campsite cleaner and better than you found it.

But I will remind you: You can't steer a parked car! Start moving so God has something to work with. After I was unwillingly without a job, I knew my next step was to begin writing the books that were on my heart. This had been a part of my calling for years, and it was time I finally did it.

But boy, did I struggle! With doubt, fear, anxiety, outlandish expectations of outcomes. I felt paralyzed. God reminded me that I just

---

[130] For more on this, see my artofthriving.net website and look at the Grace Abounds Ministries tab
[131] Albert Einstein

needed to start. Let go of expectations. Pray for guidance. But *start!* He could guide me as I went along. And He certainly did that.

There is something that every one of us could do, someplace where we would make a real difference. Let's go find it! Let's go do it.

Check out the FOWL page on the artofthriving.net website for more ideas, and to read stories, or to share your story, about women who are doing what this book suggests.

GINFWiMY*

<u>G</u>od <u>I</u>s <u>N</u>ot <u>F</u>inished <u>W</u>ith <u>M</u>e <u>Y</u>et

The book of Esther is a wonderful story, full of adventure, danger, and romance, and always worth reading again. There is a verse that always—*always*—gets me: *"And who knows but that you have come to your royal position **for such a time as this**?"*[132] This phrase could be a subtitle for this book because I truly believe that God gave you and me to the world at this time. On purpose. We have work to do.

How sad it would be if we told God no and He moved on and gave the blessing of making a difference to someone else! We are not done. God is not finished with us yet. We are not done until God says we are done. (I'm pretty sure we are not done even in heaven.) Let's be GINFWiMY Gals and be open to God's leading. Ask Him what He has for us to do. It might surprise us, but it will be good. We will make a difference. The world needs us to make a difference.

*(Pronounced: gin, with the "g" as in good; fwimmie)

---

[132] Esther 4:14

Fat Old White Lady

SECTION FOUR WORKBOOK

Core Principle: On God's Team

1. Check this list of the resources you might have to offer:
   - ❏ Talents
   - ❏ Passions
   - ❏ A lifetime of circumstances and experiences
   - ❏ Home
   - ❏ Education degrees or training
   - ❏ Skills
   - ❏ Time
   - ❏ Finances
   - ❏ Relationships
   - ❏ Spiritual maturity
   - ❏ Other _____

2. Do you have more to offer than you had thought? What could you start doing to offer your resources to be a blessing to the world and people around you?

3. In which of the spheres of influence (Media, Arts and Entertainment, Education, Government, Family, Religion and Spirituality, and Commerce / Business) have you worked in your life? Can you think of ways that someone working in each sphere could make an impact today? Which of the spheres of influence do you feel a connection to today? Is there a way you could make a difference there?

4. How are you currently acting as salt in the world around you? (Seasoning, preserving, healing, creating thirst) Where else might you be salt? How are you shining the light of Christ into the world around you? (Illuminating, warming, revealing, clarifying) Where else might you shine?

4. Have you learned what your spiritual gifts are yet? If not, what are you waiting for?

5. Are you aware of or already involved in a ministry to one of those unfortunates on Jesus' list (hungry, thirsty, a stranger, naked, in prison, or sick)? How might you take up Jesus' cause by helping someone close to His heart?

6. Have you been afflicted with the Good Girl Syndrome? What has it looked like in your life? What changes do you need to make to leave that behind? What would be different if you stopped being a Good Girl but, instead, did Good?

Well-Fed FOWL

7. Are you guilty of being over-fed but under-worked? Had you realized before that God expects you to act on what you know? Is that something you had ever considered before? Do you need to make any changes?

8. How are you blessed? Make a list of your blessings. Perhaps work on your list over a few days so it is complete. Thank God for what you find there. Perhaps make a daily or weekly gratitude list as an ongoing spiritual practice.

9. What does "blessed to be a blessing" look like in your context?

Feathering Your Nest

10. Have you been told that retirement is the time to focus on yourself? Do you think this book is right that, instead, it is a new season in which you can still be a blessing? How does that make you feel?

11. What does it mean to "store up treasures in heaven?" (Matthew 6:19-21) Have you been doing that? What does it look like in your setting, in your time of life?

The Roost

6. Do you recognize a need for control in your attitudes or approach to life? In trying to do God's will? Where could you let go, relinquish control to God?

7. Has God's will and work felt burdensome to you? In what way? How did the verse (Matthew 11:28-29) about taking up His yoke as an easy burden affect you? Did you already know this or did it cause you to see God's will in a new way? Do you need to make some changes so that your experience of God's will is light and not burdensome?

8. Before you read the section called "The right answer," how would you have answered the question it posed? How did you think you would get into heaven? Was it a shock to read that there is no way you can be good enough or do enough good to earn your way into heaven? How did you respond to reading the right answer (trusting in what Jesus did for you)? Have you done that—trusted in what God accomplished on the cross through Jesus? If not, can you do it right now?

9. Is it a relief to know that you can stop being a Good Girl?

Water FOWL

10. Are you or is your church one of those groups that have an "awkward" relationship with the Holy Spirit? How did you think of the Holy Spirit (if you ever did)? Have you had a negative experience with someone talking about the Holy Spirit or spiritual gifts? Did this chapter change your perception of or your attitude toward the Spirit? If so, how so?

11. Have you ever considered how much you need the Holy Spirit? Have you noticed a difference between work that is done merely by human hands, and work that God's Spirit was obviously empowering? Are you convinced now, after reading the chapter, that you need Him?

Laying the Golden Egg

12. Have you seen God at work in your life? Make a list of the work you have observed. How has He worked with you? (Are there attributes that characterize how He has worked in and with you? Patiently? Tenderly? Comfortingly?) Is it clear to you that He is *not* finished working within you yet?

14. Do you have a hard heart toward God and His Kingdom? Would you be willing for Him to soften it?

15. How does it make you feel to realize that God isn't finished working through you to do something for His Kingdom? That you aren't as useless as you had once thought or that your age is irrelevant in a way you had not considered before?

16. Would you consider becoming an intentional, committed intercessor for a ministry or group? If so, consider keeping a log of the prayer requests, dating each entry. Follow up to hear what God has been doing and write those answers next to the request. (This exercise can greatly increase your enthusiasm as you see God at work.) Read that online article reference about the man who interceded for the evangelism ministry of Charles Finney. Watch the movie *War Room*.

17. Do you know of children who need an "adopted" grandmother? Could you make that connection even this week? Could you do your art in the context of worship? Could you pull out your "gift of gab" to use in evangelism? Would you be willing to get training in an area that interests you so that you could do more and be more effective?

18. Are there other places you could volunteer? If you aren't already involved somewhere, make a point to do some research this week. Find a place to explore the possibilities. Maybe even start doing something the week after.

19. Have you dismissed yourself from God's work—even after you knew He'd called you? Have you repented of that? Do you need to re-engage back into the work God called you to?

20. Go through the footnoted scriptures. Look at them in the context used in this book. What did you learn? Did you change an opinion? Will you now change an action?

WHAT'S NEXT

Here's what I am hoping will happen after you read this book:
- You will:
    - Begin to cogitate, reflect, and dream
    - Get uncomfortable with the status quo
    - Meet with other women to reflect, pray — and begin to dream together
    - Come to a **FOWL Forum** near you
- If you:
    - Are wounded and damaged, you will pursue healing and find breakthrough
    - Have never worked to advance God's Kingdom, you will get excited to do something of real and eternal significance
    - Are wasting your days, marking time until you die, you will gain a sense of purpose, meaning, and fulfillment in pursuing the *Missio Dei*.
- And then you will:
    - Choose to seek God at a new level, listen to the Holy Spirit, let Him teach, guide, and empower you
    - Share this book and the FOWL Forum with your friends across the country
    - Connect with the larger FOWL community
- And finally, that enough women would work together that real work gets done, real change happens. The "sleeping giant" awakens.

APPENDIX: ABOUT GOD

Love

1 John 4:8, 10
John 3:16
Romans 5:5; 8:39
Psalm 100:5

Unchanging

Hebrews 13:8
Isaiah 40:28
Numbers 23:19

Compassionate

2 Peter 3:9
Psalm 86:15

Good

1 John 1:5
James 1:17
Psalm 103:1-22
Psalm 25:8

Forgiving

Exodus 34:6-7
Micah 17:18
John 1:29
Psalm 86:5

Helps us

John 14:26
Isaiah 41:10
Matthew 6:26
Psalms 46:1-2
Psalm 54:4
2 Samuel 22:32-34
Psalm 94:22
Genesis 22:14

Merciful and Gracious

Deuteronomy 4:31
2 Chronicles 30:9
Hebrews 4:16

APPENDIX: ABOUT US

God delights in us

Psalm 147:11
Isaiah 62:5
Psalm 18:19
Zephaniah 3:17

God loves us

Ephesians 3:17-19
Romans 5:8
John 17:23
Luke 12:6-7
John 3:16

We are His children

1 John 3:1
Galatians 4:6-7
Isaiah 49:15-16

Thinks & does good toward us

Jeremiah 29:11
Psalm 40:5
Matthew 7:9-11
Luke 12:28-31
John 10:11-13
Luke 15:11-24
Romans 8:28

Wants to bless us

Isaiah 1:19
Luke 12:32

Wants us free from sin

Isaiah 1:18
2 Corinthians 5:19
Psalm 103:10-13
Isaiah 55:7
Revelation 3:20

ORDERING

How to get the road maps, mini-books, and other resources mentioned in this book:

- Online: www.artofthriving.net. Download for free!
- By mail: For a package of all of the give-aways in hard-copy form, check the website for the address (or call 406/794-1121), and send $10 (for shipping and handling).

You can find other information and resources on the Art of Thriving website, including:

- *Grace Abounds Ministries:* This is a two-part seminar offering the ministry of transforming prayer for those needing healing *as well as* training for those who are called to become prayer ministers.

- *Books*:

    The Art of Thriving: 12 Life Skills for Living Well. A visual treat, with information that will help you bring about positive personal transformation.

    Yes! A unique approach to describing the work of God through Christ — in an adult picture-book format. Suitable for Easter or Christmas outreach.

- *LifeStory Report.* This interview-based analysis of your life experiences helps you identify your passions as well as identify your preferred work environment, use of time, reward, and working with people. Want help figuring out a good direction for work or service? This report can help.

THE FOWL FORUM

You've read the FOWL book. Now gather with other women who are interested in moving forward.

The FOWL Forum will:
- Energize, excite, and focus you
- Give you practical steps for moving forward
- Catapult you into a whole new level with God

Where to find the nearest Forum:
Go to the artofthriving.net website, calendar page.

Help host a FOWL Forum in your town or city:
It's easy. We are looking for a host organization who can help us coordinate logistics (we do much of the work) and do the inviting. There are more details online. It isn't complicated and we provide the guidance to make it work.

To schedule a FOWL forum in your town or city, contact:
France Marcott:
info@artofthriving.net
406/794-1121

www.ingramcontent.com/pod-product-compliance
Lightning Source LLC
Chambersburg PA
CBHW071505040426
42444CB00008B/1503